Sights with Stories
in Old Beijing

Panda Books

First Edition 2005

ISBN 7-119-03749-8

©Foreign Languages Press, Beijing, China, 2005

Published by Foreign Languages Press

24 Baiwanzhuang Road, Beijing 100037, China

Website: http://www.flp.com.cn

E-mail Address: info@flp.com.cn

sales@flp.com.cn

Distributed by China International Book Trading Corporation

35 Chegongzhuang Xilu, Beijing 100044, China

P.O. Box 399, Beijing, China

Printed in the People's Republic of China

Editors' Note

There is virtually no sight in Beijing that has not a fascinating story or legend attached to it, whether to do with its foundation, its architecture or the historical figures associated with it. This time-honoured local lore, still very much alive in the city, weaves marvellous tales around the natural wonders and architectural showpieces of the capital, peopling them with miraculous immortals and imaginatively embroidering their history.

Apocryphal though most of them are, they embody in their eulogy of honest toil and talent and their condemnation of wickedness a historical reality that all too often is missing from the history books themselves.

We invite you to taste through them the authentic oral literature of Beijing.

CONTENTS

A sketch map of sights mentioned in the book

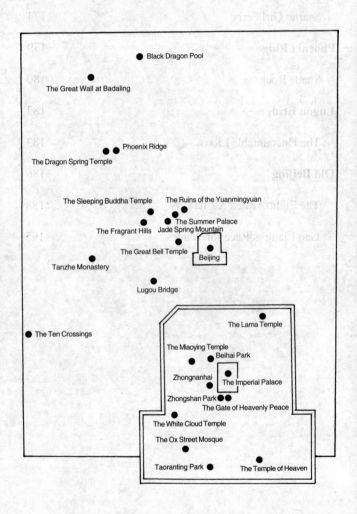

Black Dragon Pool

The Great Wall at Badaling

Phoenix Ridge

The Dragon Spring Temple

The Sleeping Buddha Temple

The Ruins of the Yuanmingyuan

The Fragrant Hills

The Summer Palace

Jade Spring Mountain

The Great Bell Temple

Beijing

Tanzhe Monastery

Lugou Bridge

The Ten Crossings

The Lama Temple

The Miaoying Temple

Beihai Park

Zhongnanhai

The Imperial Palace

Zhongshan Park

The Gate of Heavenly Peace

The White Cloud Temple

The Ox Street Mosque

Taoranting Park

The Temple of Heaven

The Temple of Heaven

THE Temple of Heaven Park, the largest remaining group of temple buildings in China, is in the southern district of Beijing. Its construction began in the fourth year (1406) of the reign of Yongle of the Ming Dynasty and ended in the eighteenth year (1420). It was the place where emperors of the Ming and Qing dynasties worshipped and prayed for good harvests. At first it had separate altars of earth and heaven. It adopted its present name during the Jiajing Period of the Ming Dynasty.

It has inner and outer altars. Its wall is circular in the north representing heaven, and square in the south representing earth, according to the age-old Chinese saying that Heaven is round and Earth square. The outer altar has fruit trees and gardens, while the inner altar has most of the buildings — the Altar for Grain Prayers in the north, the Circular Mound in the south and the Hall of Abstinence inside the western gate. A 360-metre raised causeway connects the Altar for Grain Prayers and the Altar of the Mound.

The Altar for Grain Prayers is made up of the Hall of Prayer for Good Harvest, the Hall of Imperial Heaven and the Gate of Prayer for Good Harvest. Immediately inside the gate is a three-tiered circular base with white marble balusters, occupying 5,900 square metres, on which stands a triple conical-roofed hall the well-known Hall of Prayer for Good Harvest. It is thirty-eight metres high and yellow-glazed on the roof. Inside the hall are pillars arranged in orderly rows; the inner four representing the four seasons of the year, the twelve in the middle representing the twelve months of the lunar calendar, and the outer twelve representing the twelve two-hour periods of the day. Twenty-four eave pillars stand for the twenty-four solar periods of each year. Every year, in the first month by the lunar calendar, emperors of the Ming and Qing would come here to pray for a good harvest. The Hall of Imperial Heaven to the north was where the tablets of the gods were kept.

The Circular Mound Altar refers to the Circular Mound and Imperial Vault of Heaven. It was here where emperors worshipped Heaven at the beginning of winter each year. The altar is circular and three-tiered. Ancient Chinese cosmology regards the sun as male, so the numbers of parts in a building must be male too, i.e. in odd numbers or multiples of odd numbers. A whisper at the centre of the mound sounds louder to the speaker than to the bystanders, because of sound waves bouncing from the balusters many times in succession. The Imperial Vault of Heaven, with a blue-glazed roof, is where the tablet of the God of Heaven used to be kept. Around the vault is a smooth, circular wall known as the Echoing Wall. As sound bounces off the carved wall in succession, a whisper at one point on the wall can be heard as clearly at the opposite point sixty metres off as over a telephone. In front of the vault are the Three Echoing Stones: a clap over the first stone produces a single echo, over the second a double and over the third a triple echo. Outside the northwestern wall is a 500-year-old cypress tree named the Nine Dragon Cypress.

The Hall of Abstinence is where emperors fasted before the ceremony. It is made up of a main hall, a chamber and a bell tower. The main hall is quite beamless. Before it stand bronze human figures and tablets indicating the hours. Around the Hall of Abstinence are 163 rooms. Two deep "imperial ditches" on either side of the wall indicate the extreme seclusion of the place in the past, adding more mystery to the park.

Motherwort

THE Temple of Heaven used to abound with motherwort and had many herbalists processing and dealing in the medicinal herb, for which sick women came from at over the country.

Beijing people believed the herb came from the immortals.

There used to be a village of twenty-odd households, where once an old man died leaving his wife and young daughter in poverty. Before long the old woman fell ill too. The villagers were worried, not to mention the daughter, who wept by her mother every day. When she heard that a wonder drug from the Northern Hills could cure her mother, she made up her mind to go and get some. She said to her mother before she left, "Please don't worry about me. I will return as soon as I get the herb."

"How can I let a young girl go such a long way?" said her mother, upset.

"Don't worry," the girl reassured her. "I'm old enough to take care of myself."

She asked somebody to take care of her mother, then went on her trip.

She walked and walked, thinking: "Where are the Northern Hills? They must be to the north." So she headed directly north. After three days' journey she found herself before hills with luxuriant trees and white clouds shrouding them half way up. These must be they, she thought. But where was the way up? Just as she was wondering, a white-bearded old man came from the opposite direction. She walked up and respectfully greeted him, then asked: "Are these the Northern Hills?"

The old man looked her up and down, then replied, "Yes, but why are you here?"

"My mother is seriously ill. I came for some herbs."

"Are you alone?"

"Yes."

"It is a hard trip. Go up from here, and after seven turns left and eight right you will be at Heaven on Earth, where you can get the herb. But you must be careful. Take pine seeds if you are hungry and spring water if thirsty, and return as soon as you can."

The girl hastily bowed in thanks. She raised her head only to find the old man gone. So she went into the hills following his instructions.

After seven left turns and eight right turns she was exhausted. As she sat down on a boulder she noticed a spring at her feet. She took several mouthfuls from it. Strangely, she found her mind clearer and eyes sharper. Under some weird pine trees close by, she found some pine seeds and ate them up. She felt her strength return. She got to the summit without a stop.

From the summit the view was breathtaking: green peaks and trees half visible in mist and clouds like a wonderland. In a valley was a moon-shaped pool, its crystal-clear water mirroring the clouds and distant peaks. She looked at herself in the water. To her surprise she found her face no longer racked with grief at her mother's illness but lively and ruddy. No wonder people say the Northern Hills are miraculous, she thought to herself, if even a poor girl like me has changed. The herbs here must be able to cure my mother.

Just then she heard somebody talking behind her. She turned around and saw two angelic girls walking up to her, one in white and the other in bright yellow. Plum flowers embroidered on their dresses made them even more beautiful. Where had they come from in such a remote place as this, she wondered as they approached.

The girl in white broke into a smile and addressed the daughter as "sister". Not knowing what to do, the daughter returned the same greeting. Then the girl in yellow came up and took her hand, asking, "Sister, why are you here?"

The question brought tears to the daughter's eyes. "My mother is seriously ill, and I am here for herbs. Please help me."

"Don't worry," the two girls comforted her. "We will help

you. You just stay here and rest." Then they fetched herbs from over the hill and gave them to her, saying, "Brew them for your mother. She will soon be well."

The daughter couldn't believe that she had got the herbs so easily and asked, "The old man down there told me only Heaven on Earth had the herbs. Is this the place?"

At this the two girls laughed and pointing to the moon-shaped pool said, "Is that not Heaven on Earth?"

The daughter turned around to look at the pool. It was really like the moon. Delighted, she was about to go but was stopped by the two girls: "Just a minute. Here are some seeds. Take them home and plant them. When anyone else falls ill you needn't make another trip here."

With many thanks the daughter took her leave. Some steps off she turned around. The girls were gone, but by the pine trees beside the pool she saw a crane and a deer.

The daughter hurried home and brewed the herbs, and her mother took the potion. Two days later her mother was up and about. All the villagers came to see her, but none of them could recognize the herb the daughter had brought back. An aged man said, "Since it was brought back by a daughter for her mother, why not call it 'motherwort'?"

Soon the name spread afar.

The daughter gave the seeds to the villagers to plant. Some opened shops selling the herbs, and the village became known throughout the country as "Motherwort Village".

Soon, when the Emperor planned to build the Temple of

Heaven, he was told that the village was an auspicious place and that if the temple were built there good harvests would be guaranteed every year. So the emperor fenced the place in for the construction.

Buildings were put up, and the motherwort kept growing. One day when the Emperor came to worship heaven his anger rose at the sight of so many weeds. He ordered his men to root them out. Just then the white-bearded old man reappeared, and with a few whisks of his duster all the motherwort turned into dragon-hair grass, whereupon he disappeared again.

Those working on the weeds immediately reported to the emperor what had happened. The Emperor said, "The dragon-hair grass is not to be touched." So the weeds were protected.

Actually it was still motherwort, which when it is small looks like dragon-hair grass but not when fully grown.

The Wedges in the Hall of Prayer for Good Harvest

OVER a thousand workers were working hard to build the hall when one day an old man of about seventy came claiming that he was a carpenter and asked for work. The supervisor took pity on him and told him to work for Carpenter Liu, who took the old man to his yard but continued with his own job. After a while the old man asked, "What is my job?"

Carpenter Liu glanced at him impatiently and said, "Work on this." And he kicked the old man a log about twenty centimetres long. He didn't explain further; neither did the old man ask any more questions. He just carried the log away and began working on it. He worked a whole day, drawing numerous lines on all sides of it.

The next day, when work had already begun, the old man hadn't shown up. Carpenter Liu said angrily, "What the hell was he doing here?"

He went to where the old man had worked. "What a waste," he said, and gave the log a kick, at which it fell into wedges, each of which was numbered. When his surprise had passed Carpenter Liu understood: they must have been left by Master Lu Ban*, and for a purpose.

The hall was almost finished, but while the workers installed the roof they found the joints between the columns and beams not fast enough. Carpenter Liu thought of the wedges, which he tried on the joints. They fitted perfectly! When he had put in the last wedge the roof was done. "How did you know to prepare those wedges in advance?" he was asked, and he told them about the old man, to whom everybody was grateful.

---

* Lu Ban, a master carpenter in the Warring States Period, was worshipped subsequently by all in the trade.

Heaven's Heart Stone

AN emperor in his majesty was unhappy, even though his ministers kept to and tried hard to please him.

"I am carrying out the way of Heaven," one day he said to his prime minister. "Wherever I go I should find response, even from Heaven. Can you achieve that for me?"

"We must follow Heaven's heart. Why not get a heaven's heart stone and set it on a mound? Your Majesty shall stand on it, and your voice will be answered by Heaven."

"Yes!" said the Emperor, and sent an official all over the country to bring him such a stone.

Far as he travelled, the official could find no "heaven's heart stone". One day, while passing Mount Wutai, he saw an old stonemason working on a piece of stone. He was carving a turtle and cloud pattern on it.

"What stone is this?" the official asked.

"Heaven's Star Stone," the mason answered.

The official misunderstood this as "heaven's heart stone" and immediately asked, "Where is it from?"

"Right here, from Mount Wutai."

The official was wild with joy. He asked again,

"What are you carving?"

"A turtle."

"For whom?"

"The court."

The official's joy was beyond words. "You needn't work on it any more. The Emperor wants it immediately. Go with me now."

"What about the turtle?" asked the mason diffidently.

"Don't worry about that. You may bring it along." With these words he took the old mason away.

In Beijing the official reported to the prime minister about his trip, claiming that he had found the "heaven's heart stone".

The prime minister's face fell when he saw the stone turtle. "What I want is 'heaven's heart stone', not a stone turtle," he shouted.

"The mason said this was the stone," the official protested.

"Then where is the mason? Sent for him immediately."

When the old stonemason was brought to the prime minister, he said, "This is 'Heaven's Star Stone' from Mount Wutai, and I was carving on it a turtle."

The prime minister misheard him too, so he sent someone to Mount Wutai for the stone and began to build a circular mound.

It was a unique mound: nine stones formed the centre, eighteen stones the second ring and twenty-seven another ring, nine and multiples of nine because of the "nine provinces under Heaven", so that the mound should be the centre of the universe to manifest the imperial power.

When the mound was done the prime minister came to inspect it. He climbed to the top and looked down and really felt he was at the centre of the universe. He cried aloud but failed to produce any echo.

He was worried. "Why didn't it echo?" he asked the old mason.

"It will if you build walls around it."

So the prime minister ordered walls built immediately. As the mound was three-tiered, so would be the walls. He built another one round in the south and square in the north, for Heaven is round and Earth is square.

After this he shouted again. Sure enough, echoes were produced.

Even now people visiting the Temple of Heaven try the wall: some clap their hands to hear the echo; lovers go there to pledge their love; aged people and foreigners murmur a prayer, but most just shout to enjoy the echo.

The Imperial Palace

THE Imperial Palace, also known in the past as the Forbidden City and the palace of the Ming and Qing dynasties, is located in the heart of Beijing and is the biggest and the most intact of the extant architectural complexes in China. Construction of the palace began in the fourth year (1406) of the Yongle reign of the Ming and was completed fourteen years later. Twenty-four emperors of the Ming and Qing dynasties lived here. With a history of more than five hundred and sixty years, the palace occupies an area of 720,000 square metres with more than 9,000 buildings. The wall around it extends about three kilometres. At each corner of the wall is an exquisite and stylistic watch-tower, and outside the wall is a moat. All these come together to form a strongly fortified castle. The Imperial Palace is divided into the "outer court" and the "inner court". The Hall of Supreme Harmony, the Hall of Central Harmony and the Hall of Preserved Harmony are the centre of the "outer court", and on either side of them are the Hall of Literary Glory and the Hall of Martial Valour.

These are main buildings where the Emperor conducted important ceremonies, received his subjects and exercised his rule over the state. Inside the "inner court" are the Palace of Celestial Purity, the Hall of Celestial and Terrestrial Union, the Hall of Earthly Tranquillity and six palaces on either side of them. These places are where the Emperor conducted everyday affairs and where his concubines and children lived.

The Imperial Palace, with its grand and magnificent buildings, is the essence of ancient Chinese architecture and a precious cultural heritage of the Chinese people; and it is now a scenic spot that tourists are bound to visit.

The Red-Crowned Crane in the Chuxiu Palace

THERE are six palaces in the east part and six palaces in the west part of the Imperial Palace complex. The Chuxiu Palace is one of the six palaces in the west. A bronze red-crowned crane is in front of the Chuxiu Palace. An arrow wound can be seen on the left leg of the red-crowned crane.

The legend goes like this: the red-crowned crane was once wild. He flew to the Imperial Palace to ingratiate himself with the Emperor Qianlong, so he stayed by him all day long. One day, he said to Qianlong with out-stretched neck, "Your Majesty, you are the most blessed emperor in the world. I flew here specially from the southern mountains to wait on you." Glancing at him, Qianlong wondered where this wild crane was from and did not pay any attention to him. When he saw Qianlong leaving, he hurriedly caught up with him and said with a deep bow, "Your Majesty, I can sound the night watches for you and escort you." Glancing at him again, Qianlong said impatiently, "Then you can just stay in front of the Chuxiu Palace." So he stayed there from then on.

Before long, the Emperor Qianlong went to the south with his retinue. His favourite place in the south was Hangzhou. He loved hunting, so he went hunting soon after he arrived there. The crane could no longer remain where he was now that Qianlong had left. He thought: "What's the use of my sounding the night watches, since Qianlong is not here? Why don't I go to the south to escort him and at the same time curry favour with him?" At this thought, he stretched his neck, tidied his feathers and flew in the direction of Hangzhou.

That day, Qianlong was hunting in informal dress on a big horse, followed by his retinue. When he caught sight of Qianlong, the red-crowned crane thought: "This is a good chance. It will certainly make His Majesty happy if I prostrate myself before him, saying I'm here to escort him and guide his hunt." With this in mind, he flew up into the sky and made for Qianlong. Qianlong saw a big bird flying towards him. "I'll just have a try," he said. So he took out an arrow, put it to the bow and shot. The red-crowned crane was greatly alarmed and said, "Your Majesty, it's me, it's me!" But the arrow was already on its way. The crane was shot in the left leg and dropped down to the ground. When Qianlong rode up to him, the red-crowned crane kowtowed and said, "Your Majesty, I came here specially to escort you." Qianlong became angry when he realized it was the wild crane and said, "I told you to sound the night watches in the Chuxiu Palace. I never wanted you to escort me! Go away!" The red-crowned crane flew back without a word.

The red-crowned crane stayed in front of the Chuxiu Palace again when he got back to the Imperial Palace. However, the wound on his left leg remained there for ever. All those who saw it said it served him right.

Four Stone Lions

TWO stone lions sit on the top of the ornamental columns in front of Tian'anmen, formerly named the Gate for Receiving Orders from Heaven. Another two stone lions sit on the similar columns at the end of the Marco Polo Bridge. The former face north, and the latter look to the east.

Legend has it that one year a severe famine fell on the land, and the authorities forced all able-bodied men to be warriors. Everywhere were cries and moans of bitterness and sorrow, which only grew louder at night, but the Emperor had never cared about state affairs in all his reign. Instead he played chess and drank with the concubines, enjoying their performances. Tons of government documents from his ministers piled up on his desk.

Yet the people cried so loud that it reached the imperial palace. It angered the Emperor, who ordered that whoever cried next was to have his head chopped off. When the people heard the imperial edict they sobbed in secret.

Days later, another wave of cries reached the palace from

above. Annoyed, the Emperor sent his eunuch to investigate. When the eunuch walked out of Tian'anmen Gate he heard cries from above his head. He lifted his head and found it was the ornamental animals on the roof ridges of the rostrum that were crying. They had witnessed the suffering of the people and could not help crying too.

At that time the gate-tower was more than 33 metres high and had 36 windows and doors. There were lines of ornamental animals standing on the main ridge as well as the four supporting ridges: an owl-like bird, a dragon, a phoenix, a lion, a sky horse, a seahorse, a fish and two legendary animals called *xie* and *shen*. The owl-like bird was a ready moaner, like the people.

The eunuch reported it to the Emperor. "Whoever is the leader, get him!" ordered the emperor. As soon as the eunuch set up the ladder and was ready to climb onto the roof of the tower, the bird flew away from the Forbidden City. He chased it and found the miserable subjects moaning at the foot of the palace wall.

Then the two stone lions on the top of the ornamental columns could not stand it any more and called: "Oh, Your Majesty, do not always stay in the palace and live in decadence with the concubines; come out quickly and take a look at the suffering people." They repeated their plea.

It really annoyed the Emperor, who finally came out of the palace. From then on the two stone lions have been called the Callers of the Emperor.

When the Emperor saw the people crying by his wall he ordered them dispersed. Then he left the capital for the south with some intimate ministers.

It was springtime when they got to the south, where green hills and blue waters abound with singing birds and blooming flowers. They visited Yangzhou, Suzhou and Hangzhou, intoxicated by their picturesque scenery and beautiful women.

Then the dragon and the phoenix flew away too, and the palace became desolate, for which the concubines cursed Heaven and Earth and swore at the lions particularly.

But the two stone lions at the end of the Marco Polo Bridge stretched their necks into the air and looked into the distance all day for the Emperor. When they became impatient they roared loudly to the south.

A few days passed, and the Emperor was still nowhere to be seen. The lions turned and roared to the river underneath: "Your Majesty, Your Majesty, how dissolute you are! The country will be no more if you finger there!"

Their voices shook heaven and earth, traversed the waves and clouds and reached the south. The Emperor heard them and returned to the capital. Taking his ministers' advice, he began to take care of state affairs.

The Marco Polo Bridge lions were named the Watchers of the Emperor.

The Watch-towers

THE Forbidden City is a square brick city, on whose four corners are four watch-towers, each of them with nine roof beams, eighteen pillars and seventy-two ridgepoles. These watchtowers are ingeniously constructed and pleasant to the eye. But who designed them?

It is said that when the city of Beijing was built there were no watch-towers, only the tall, thick red wall. One night, the Emperor had dreamed of a city with four towers standing at its corners, more delightful than he had ever seen before. Waking, he ordered that four watch-towers like those he had dreamed of should be built at the four corners of the Forbidden City.

The Minister of Works received the imperial edict and summoned craftsmen from every corner of the country to build the four watch-towers in three months, just as the Emperor had seen them in his dream, with nine roof beams, eighteen pillars and seventy-two ridgepoles.

The manager of one of the eight state wood mills accepted

the job without any hesitation, and in three months four watch-towers were completed. The Minister of Works inspected them and found that they were painted golden and carved, and with their upturned eaves looked right, so he presented a memorial to the Emperor and asked him to inspect them. Seeing them, the Emperor said that they were nothing like what he had dreamed of, so he killed the manager. Another manager of another mill was more careful, and with his thirty best craftsmen set to work: the frames were very impressive, and with their golden roofs and red eaves they looked like four exquisite pagodas. In three months they completed their work. The emperor examined them and said that as they hadn't put in nine roof beams, eighteen pillars and seventy-two ridgepoles, they had committed lèse-majesté, and he killed the manager and the thirty craftsmen.

The third mill had already prepared itself. Every day they brooded over the nine roof beams, eighteen pillars and seventy-two ridgepoles. The manager was so worried that he could neither eat nor sleep. It was then the heat of sumraer, and they were almost out of breath, so that what with their anxiety and anger, each of them was weak. When it came to the noon nap, all went to find cool places to sleep.

One day they were lying there and gossiping when the music of grasshoppers came to their ears, easing their minds. One of the apprentices couldn't help going out to look: an old man with a shoulder pole was selling grasshoppers, but the price was extremely high. Some days later, at noon, the grass-

hoppers sang louder and louder, and the apprentice was fed up. He went out to complain. The old man said, "How can a grasshopper keep silent?" The little apprentice argued with the old man, and all of the craftsmen came up to them. Seeing them approach, the old man held high his grasshopper cage and said loudly, "Masters, won't you buy my fine grasshopper in his fine cage?" All the craftsmen fixed their eyes on the cage, and someone shouted:

"Nine roof beams, eighteen pillars and seventy-two ridgepoles!" Suddenly all was clear.

The cage was beautifully woven of thin sorghum stalks with eight sides and eight more at every corner. The roof was divided into three storeys the first had upturned eaves on its four sides, and each of the four corners also had four small upturned caves; the second was very much like the first, except that on its four small upturned eaves were four triangular ridgepoles; like the second, the third had four triangular ridgepoles, but on the ridgepoles were four more triarigular ridgepoles, and on each of them stood four level ridgepoles.

The craftsmen built the watch-towers according to this structure, and the Emperor was satisfied after inspecting them. And who was that old man selling grasshoppers? None other than Lu Ban.

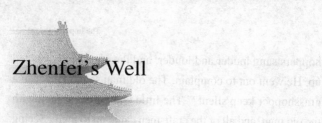

Zhenfei's Well

IN the eastern and western courtyards in the Imperial Palace there are wells with beautiful pavilions over them and surrounded by jade railings, which are called the Eight Treasures Coloured Glaze Wells. Yet another, stone-edged well, small and lonely with neither pavilion nor jade railings, is more famous. This is Zhenfei's Well. All Beijingers know the following legend about it.

It is so called after Zhenfei, a concubine of the Emperor Guangxu of the Qing Dynasty, because she was drowned in it. Zhenfei had a sister named Jinfei, who was two years older than she, and both were selected to enter the court as concubines of Guangxu.

Although Guangxu was emperor, he was a puppet controlled by the Empress Dowager Cixi from the day he came to the throne. Growing up and finding his country weak and always cheated and insulted by foreign countries, he thought to make her rich and strong. At that time, some ministers and literati wanted to carry out reforms, which he supported, as did Zhenfei, who helped him in every aspect, and Guangxu liked her very much.

But the Empress Dowager Cixi hated Guangxu for his views on reform and especially hated Zhenfei for her support of him. She summoned Zhenfei, railing at her, "You contemptible wretch! If you continue to support this, I'll have your skin off!" Zhenfei said, "Reform would be a good thing. He is my husband, and I can't stand idle." Hardly were the words out than the Empress Dowager Cixi slapped her face, saying with rage, "You two are man and wife, and I'll never let you see each other again!" After that Zhenfei was consigned to limbo and was not allowed to see the Emperor Guangxu.

The limbo was a small courtyard in the southeastern corner of the Imperial Palace, isolated from the outside world. Although she was provided with food, she was getting thinner with every passing day. Her sister Jinfei had nothing to do with the reforms, but she was often scolded because of Zhenfei. Seeing Zhenfei consigned to limbo, she felt extremely uneasy. Sometimes she stealthily delivered clothes to her and sometimes comforting words. Hers was the only kindness Zhenfei felt.

In 1900, when the Allied Forces of the Eight Powers invaded Beijing, the Empress Dowager Cixi, greatly terrified, planned to flee with Guangxu, but what was to be done about Zhenfei? To take her would have been to let her off lightly, to leave her behind future trouble. The best way was to order her to commit suicide. The Empress Dowager entrusted the affair to the Second Manager.

The Second Manager, nicknamed Murderous Ghost, came to the small courtyard, and announced the order to Zhenfei, who was not convinced and was brought before the Empress Dowager, cursing all the way. The Empress Dowager flew into a rage and ordered, "Be quick! Push her down the well!"

When the Second Manager carried Zhenfei to one of the Eight Treasures Coloured Glaze Wells, she clutched the jade railings and kicked him when he tried to bind her hands. He had to carry her back to the lonely well and push her down with all his strength. Then he found a round stone and covered the well with it. When he hurried back to report, the Empress Dowager had already fled through the Gate of Divine Might, heading for Xi'an.

Zhenfei was drowned. Her body remained in the well for more than a year. All the maids in the palace were sad, and they helped Jinfei arrange a mourning hall in a house opposite the well. Later people called the well Zhenfei's Well in her memory. It is said that even now you can hear her cries in the well if you bend over it at night.

The Great Wall at Badaling

A magnificent construction in ancient China and the largest defensive project in the world, the Great Wall began to be built in the 7th century BC, when rival feudal kingdoms built walls around their territories for self-protection. The high walls built by the three kingdoms of Qin, Zhao and Yan as a defence against nomadic tribes in the north laid the foundations of the present Great Wall. Following unification of the separate kingdoms under Qin Shi Huang (the First Emperor of the Qin) in 221 BC, the existing walls were linked up and extended.

Subsequent dynasties continued to strengthen and extend the wall. The Ming Dynasty, in order to secure its territory from Mongol and Nüzhen forces, replaced the old wall of stones and clay with evenly sized stone blocks and bricks and extended the wall to 6,700 kilometres long, from Jiayuguan Pass in the west to Shanhaiguan Pass in the east. Along the wall many beacon towers were erected to warn of an enemy's advance with smoke during the day and fire at night.

The magnificent old Great Wall has drawn numerous Chinese and foreign tourists. Badaling, one of its fortresses, is termed "the strategic north". Built in the 18th year (1505) of the Hongzhi Period of the Ming, it has two gates, which command the Beijing-Zhangjiakou highway. The fortress is flanked by the undulating Great Wall, winding among mountains like a huge dragon. With many outposts, and differing in thickness from four to five metres and in height from six to seven metres, the Great Wall makes a breathtaking spectacle.

The Northern Tribes Destroying Qin

WHY did Qin Shi Huang build the Great Wall? There is a story attached.

After his unification of the separate kingdoms, Qin Shi Huang enjoyed nationwide peace and a luxurious life, accompanied by beautiful women and excellent wine. One day, overwhelmed by a sudden worry of death and the loss of his power and wealth, he decided to get the elixir of immortality.

A man named Lu Sheng, in order to please Qin Shi Huang and make some money out of him, claimed to associate with immortals and volunteered to make a trip. Overjoyed, Qin Shi Huang gave him a lot of gold and silver to finance it. Several days later Lu Sheng returned, saying that he had been to a fairyland and seen many immortals, all of whom had the elixir, but that as his visit was untimely he had been embarrassed to ask for any, though he had got a book from them.

Qin Shi Huang could not understand the few words in the book, but he was startled by the line "nomadic tribes destroying Qin". Why not forestall them while Qin was powerful?

So he dispatched several hundred thousand troops on the mission.

In fact Lu Sheng had never seen any immortals. He had just cheated Qin Shi Huang out of money.

As disaster fell, the unprepared northern tribes fled from their grasslands and livestocks to places Qin's army could not reach.

Qin Shi Huang knew his unprovoked attack would incur revenge, so he ordered a strong wall to be built to keep out the nomadic forces.

That is why the Great Wall was begun.

Meng Jiangnü

TRADITION has it that in the Qin Dynasty (221-206 BC) there were two families who lived next door to each other, neither with any children. For many years they had got along very well together.

One year the Meng family planted a melon seed that grew and grew. The vine climbed over the wall, and a melon appeared. The melon grew bigger and bigger day by day. The two families treasured it dearly. In the autumn it ripened. As the melon belonged to both families, it had to be cut in half, but when it was opened, to their surprise, a pretty little girl with big eyes sat inside. The two families were both astonished and happy. She was given the name Meng Jiangnü (the Girl of the Mengs and Jiangs).

When Meng Jiangnü grew up, she was as beautiful as a flower. Intelligent, clever and hardworking, she could weave at home and pick mulberry leaves in the fields. All her neighbours praised her.

When it was time for her to get engaged, matchmakers

flowed to her house. The two old couples considered at length and finally fixed their choice on a young man named Wan Xiliang, who was very handsome and capable, but the two young people still had not met.

At that time Emperor Qin Shi Huang was building the Great Wall. It was a big project, so a lot of people were needed. Any people who refused to go would be beheaded, so many young people were pressganged into building the Great Wall, and there was no set time for their return.

One evening Meng Jiangnü was embroidering pillowcases with mandarin ducks at home. She hummed a song as she did so. Suddenly the neighing of horses startled her. "They are pressganging young people again," she said to herself, as she went into the courtyard to look. As she turned her head she spotted a dark figure under the grapevine trellis, which gave her a start. "Who's that?" she cried. Before her voice had died away, a young man appeared, who said politely, "Sorry to frighten you, miss. I'm Wan Xiliang. The soldiers are after me to pressgang me into building the Great Wall. I've come to say goodbye to my uncles and aunts."

Meng Jiangnü had not met Wan Xiliang before. By the moonlight she looked him up and down and was happy to find him a handsome young man, but she was not sure he was Wan Xiliang, so she called out toward the house, "Dad!" Old Meng and his wife came out, and so did the old couple from the neighbouring house.

At the sight of their son-in-law, the old couples let him in, both worried and anxious, not knowing what to do to rescue him. Just then the clamour of people shouting and horses neighing was heard again, and flames lit up the sky. "Catch Wan Xiliang! Don't let him get away!" roared a voice.

Wan Xiliang threw himself before Old Meng and Old Jiang and kowtowed to them, and then turned to bow to Meng Jiangnü. "I must leave quickly now," he said, "or I'll get you into trouble too." With that he turned to leave.

"That's hurling yourself into the net!" Old Meng grasped him by the arm. After thinking a while, he said, "In troubled times like this, we won't live in peace any more. Since you and our daughter are engaged, it's better for you to get married tonight. Early tomorrow morning we'll send you out to find a place to hide." Old Jiang nodded his head, and Wan Xiliang and Meng Jiangnü gave their tacit consent.

So Wan Xiliang and Meng Jianguü got married that same night.

Early the next morning, when the bride and bridegroom were still sleeping in their bridal chamber, the door was kicked open, and in rushed a group of soldiers, who seized Wan Xiliang and took him away.

Wan Xiliang struggled to turn back. "Meng Jiangnü," he said, "although we've been husband and wife for only one night, our love is deeper than the ocean. Now I've been pressganged into building the Great Wall and probably won't come back again. You must take care of yourself." This said, he burst into tears.

Meng Jiangnü wept bitterly. After a moment she said to comfort her husband, "You must take care of yourself too, Xiliang, when you go to the Great Wall. I hope you'll come back in a few years." She removed a jade hairpin from her head and broke it into two. "My heart is as pure as this jade hairpin. You take half of it with you. It will remind you of me when you look at it. I hope we will meet soon." Then she walked ten miles with him before they finally parted.

Time flew. Soon it was late autumn, and wildgeese began to return south. Watching the southbound birds, Meng Jiangnü missed her husband very much. She worked hard day and night making padded clothes for him. When everything was ready she bade goodbye to her parents and took to the road to look for her husband.

She travelled for many days through numerous difficulties and finally reached the construction site of the Great Wall. She saw huge crowds of people labouring hard to carry large bricks on to the precipitous mountain ridges. One false step would send them rolling down into the deep valleys dead. Meng Jiangnü was filled with grief. She asked for Wan Xiliang everywhere, but nobody knew him.

An officer came up with a group of soldiers. When he saw Meng Jiangnü, he seized her and said with a sneer, "You still haven't forgotten Wan Xiliang, eh?"

Meng Jiangnü recognized him. "It was you who pressganged my husband," she cried. "Where is he now?"

"He's at the foot of Jiaoshan Mountain beside the Bohai

Sea."

Meng Jiangnü headed for the sea. At dusk she reached a hill with the billowing sea beyond it and undulating mountain ranges before it. "Wan Xiliang! Wan Xiliang!" she called out at the top of her lungs, but there was no reply. She searched among the crowds of labourers, but there was no trace of him there either. Finally she came upon a young man from her own village, who said to her in tears, "You are too late, Meng Jiangnü."

"What's happened to Wan Xiliang?" asked Meng Jiangnü.

"He died of exhaustion three days ago. His body was taken to fill in the foot of the Great Wall."

This news struck Meng Jiangnü like a bolt out of the blue. She cried loudly for three days and three nights until the sky dimmed and darkened the earth. On the third day the Great Wall collapsed with a crash for eight hundred *li*, and many corpses of labourers fell out. When Meng Jiangnü found her husband's corpse, the half of the jade hairpin was still in his hand. She cried for a long time before she had her husband buried.

Burning with wrath, Meng Jiangnü walked slowly to the sea and cried: "Heaven, open your eyes and see how we poor people are suffering! O vast sea, turn and listen to our grievance! Sisters, when shall we see the light of day?" With that, she jumped into the billowing sea and was quickly swallowed up.

So today in the sea southeast of Shanhaiguan Pass there

stand two huge rocks, one of which looks like a tomb and the other like a gravestone. They are called Meng Jiangnü's Mausoleum. Flocks of wildgeese perch on them wailing at night or fly circling around. This has become known as the Goose Formation at Meng Jiangnü's Tomb.

One Night too Many

IN order to finish the Great Wall early, Qin Shi Huang made thousands of people toil night and day, but he still thought the work was going on too slowly. Get more hands? Impossible, because there were no more. He thought and thought and finally hit upon an idea; if he fixed the sun at the zenith it would always be daytime, and the workers could be justifiably kept working.

He felt he could command the sun in his capacity of emperor and dragon son of heaven. That night he had a dream: he was in the house of the Sun God, but it could not match his palaces for magnificence. It was only a mill. A little gold horse was grinding gold beans on the millstone, around which a rooster circled chasing a hen. Qin Shi Huang had no interest in gold beans, as he was too wealthy. His eyes fell on the silly rooster, who was forever half a circle behind the hen. Impatiently, he put out his arms and caught the two birds, unaware that the rooster was none other than the Sun God and the hen the Moon Goddess. They had circled the millstone at an even speed from time immemorial. As their routine was dislocated, a day was missed and replaced by a night. Contrary to Qin Shi Huang's wishes, he had given the workers one more night to sleep.

The Gingko Tree

A huge gingko tree in Siqiaozi Village on the west side of the Beijing-Zhangjiakou Railway is over thirty metres high and thick enough for five people to hold it with outstretched arms. It is the king of trees and one of the tourist attractions of Guangou, a valley east of Badaling.

Legend has it that the tree was owned by a poor native of Shanxi surnamed Kang, who made a living by doing odd jobs. Once he found a place where the grass was unusually lush. He cut a load of it about a hundred *jin*, in no time. The grass was much sought after, because sick or old livestock recovered and became strong and young if they had it. Most of all, after he had cut it — and he always took no more or no less than a hundred *jin* — the grass grew immediately to its original height. One day, after cutting, he dug in the soil with his sickle. To his surprise he found a vase the size of a basin. He took it home and put in all his money, half filling it. The next morning he found the money had filled the vase. He was wild with joy. He kept putting in some money every evening, each time a little less, and got a whole vase of it next morning. He soon became very rich.

One day he found the vase was dirty, so he emptied the money from it and began to wash it. The vase was then clean, but its magic power was gone. The next morning he found the few pieces of silver he had put in the night before had not increased. Upset, Rich Man Kang washed it again in the hope of retrieving its magic power. As he put in more water he saw a huge tree mirrored in it, every branch and leaf distinct. He immediately sent for all the painters of the area to copy the tree, then he sent his men all over the country with the copy to find the real tree.

One of his men came to Guangou, where he saw a lot of trees, among them a huge one that was most impressive. He took out the copy and compared it. They were exactly the same. He was overjoyed, as Rich Man Kang had promised a big reward to whoever found the tree. But how would he prove he had found it? He hung his umbrella on the north branch and got a person from the nearby village to keep an eye on the tree until he came back. Then he rushed back to report to Rich Man Kang. It took him a fortnight to get home. Rich Man Kang jumped for joy. As the token of the Kangs' fortune, the tree must be kept intact. He set off to Guangou immediately with a lot of money. As soon as he got to the village he bought the plot and hired hands to build a wall around the tree and guard it. Rewarding each family in the village, he went home.

Three years later the north branch of the tree was broken in a gust of wind. Seeing this from the reflection in the vase, Rich Man Kang immediately sent his men to fix the branch. Six months later the tree had recovered its luxuriance. It stands erect there even today.

The Summer Palace

THE Summer Palace on the northwestern outskirts of Beijing is one of the most famous parks in China. Originally it was an imperial palace and park. In 1153 the ruler of the Jin built a temporary palace here called the Jinshan Temporary Palace. In the Ming Dynasty it was changed into an imperial garden. In 1702 the Qing emperor Kangxi enlarged it into a temporary palace, and in 1750 the Qing emperor Qianlong reconstructed it and called it the Park of Clear Ripples. In 1850 an Anglo-French joint force took Beijing and set fire to the park and burned it down. In 1888 the Empress Dowager Cixi diverted funds earmarked for the navy and restored the park, renaming it Yiheyuan, but when the Allied Forces of the Eight Powers took Beijing in 1900, the park was severely damaged once again. Restoration was carried out in 1903.

Its main features are Longevity Hill and Kunming Lake. The whole park occupies 290 hectares, with more than three thousand bays of various buildings in different palace and garden architectural styles. Buildings such as the

Tower of Buddhist Incense, the Deheyuan Theatre and the Hall of Dispelling Clouds are representative of late-Qing wooden buildings. The park's natural beauty is set off by a multitude of highly decorative halls, towers, galleries, pavilions, kiosks and bridges.

The Legend of Longevity Hill

LONGEVITY Hill in the Summer Palace was called Jar Hill before 1751. An interesting story is told about it in the western suburbs of Beijing.

A long, long time ago Jar Hill was surrounded by springs, and there was a marsh around it. The local people earned a living by fishing, brick-making or peddling wares. Except for a few rich men, they led a hard life, often short of food. They had to struggle hard.

Half way up Jar Hill there was a small dilapidated temple, in which Marshal Zhao, the God of Wealth, was worshipped. At the sight of the poor people at the foot of the hill, Marshal Zhao took pity on them and decided to make his presence felt by helping one house hold out on April 15 every year.

Sure enough, for several years running, there would be a poor man who became rich all of a sudden at the temple fair on April 15. First the hired hand Blacky Zhao dug up a jar of gold from the earth, next the soya milk seller Blindman Wang discovered a jar of silver ingots on a road, and then the fisherman Zhang the Third got a jar of pearls from the water. This news spread quickly to the ears of rich men and high officials, who began to feel very jealous. On April 15 they changed into rags and, each with a rope of coarse cloth tied around his waist and a bag slung over his shoulders, went to the temple fair. Pretending to be poor men, they wandered about here and there in the hope that Marshal Zhao, the God of Wealth, would come to aid them.

Among them there was a very rich man called Wang Youcai living to the southwest of Jar Hill. Not only did he own three hectares of land in the countryside, but also he ran several shops in the city of Beijing. He elbowed his way through the crowds at the temple fair, praying: "God of Wealth, be kind and come to help me. My eighty-year-old mother is starving nearly to death at home!" He walked from east to west and from south to north thirty-six times but never met the god. Finally he was so fatigued that he got a sore back and aching legs and went home dejected.

Once at home Wang Youcai drank two cups of tea and fell asleep on his *kang*. In a dream he saw two boys, one fat and one thin, walking out of the Temple of the God of Wealth. They were the same height and wore the same red undergarment. As they skipped along over the hill, the fat one told the thin one: "The master told us to give the jar of gold beads to the poorest man. Let's hurry and dig it up." "Who'll be the poorest man then?" asked the thin boy. "The master's found him after a year of investigation," the fat boy answered. "The man is called Old Li and lives on the western side of the hill. He has a child with a mole near one of its eyebrows. The master told us to bury the gold beads in a corner of Old Li's western room." The two little boys walked to a big pine tree over the hill and dug up a jar of shining gold beads. The thin boy bent to pick the jar up, but in his carelessness he broke off a small piece from the jar. He threw the piece on the ground, took up the jar and left. Seeing the treasure being taken away, Wang Youcai got so worried that he began to shout loudly and woke up.

Jumping off the *kang*, he ran to the pine tree, and sure enough found a piece of pottery, which looked exactly the same size as the one he had seen in his dream. He picked it up and put it into his pocket, racking his brains for how to find Old Li and dig up that jar of gold beads.

Early the next morning Wang Youcai came to search for the child with a mole near one of its eyebrows in the places around the Green Dragon Bridge to the west of Jar Hill. He searched everywhere in vain. Very disappointed, he turned to go home.

On his way home he met a man wearing rags, who was selling glutinous-rice cakes at the western end of Green Dragon Bridge Village. A glance at the man told him that he was a very poor man. Wang Youcai walked up to the man and bought a cake from him, then asked: "What's your name?" "People call me Old Li," the man answered. Pleased beyond words, Wang Youcai asked again: "How old is your child?"

Old Li sighed. "To tell you the truth, I was a bachelor for many years and married when I was forty. Now I'm nearly fifty, but I still don't know the joy of being a father."

Just then a boy ran up from the village street, shouting to him breathlessly: "Uncle, go home quick! Auntie's given birth to a fat baby boy!"

Hearing the news, Old Li dashed home happily without taking his cake barrow back, so when he came back for it, Wang Youcai still stood there looking after it for him.

"Congratulations, Old Li," said Wang Youcai.

"Is it a fat baby?"

"A very lovely boy," Old Li smiled. "He's a mole near one of his eyebrows."

"Ha! He's the one I'm looking for!" Wang Youcai said to himself. Then he set to to flatter Old Li: "The mole is a good symbol."

Old Li pushed his barrow home, and Wang Youcai followed him to his door to note the place.

A few days later Wang Youcai went to visit Old Li, taking with him a box of cakes and two bottles of wine to congratulate him on having a baby son. Old Li treated him to a meal. Thenceforth they saw each other quite often.

Once Old Li's house collapsed during a downpour. Wang Youcai said to Old Li, "I have a house in my ancestral graveyard. Would you and your family like to move in there and give me this place of yours?"

"Yes," said Old Li. "My whole family will thank you."

As soon as Old Li's family moved out, Wang Youcai entered the collapsed house and started digging in the corner of the western room to find the jar of gold beads. He dug hard and finally found the small jar. He took the piece of pottery out of his pocket, and sure enough, it fitted the missing part of the jar. But when he removed the cover, vipers came out, coiled around him and bit him, and soon Wang Youcai was dead.

Old Li moved back to Green Dragon Bridge. When he rebuilt his house, he dug up a pottery jar full of gold beads.

Ever since then the hill has been known as Jar Hill.

Kunming Lake

IN ancient times Longevity Hill was known as Jar Hill, and Kunming Lake as Jar Hill Pond. How did the ordinary hill and lake become a famous imperial park?

Tradition has it that during the Liao and Jin dynasties Jar Hill was a nearly barren hill with a solitary temple on the top. In the temple lived an old monk, whose age no one knew.

When the Mongols rose to power, their leader Genghis Khan led his men to capture Beijing. They were billeted in Haidian in the northwestern suburbs. One day Genghis Khan went hunting with his men in the Western Hills. Yelü Chucai, who had surrendered to him, suggested that Jar Hill would be the best place. He asked Genghis Khan to leave his men at the foot of the hill, and he and Genghis Khan went together to the temple on the hilltop. The old monk made a bow to them and then stood aside. When Genghis Khan asked him his age and the name of the hill, he just said he was deaf. Enraged, Genghis Khan drew his sword to kill him. Yelü Chucai stopped him quickly, intimating with a wink that the

old monk was not to be trifled with. He secretly ordered their troops to surround the hill, while he and Genghis Khan pitched leather tents not far from the temple.

At midnight, as Genghis Khan and Yelü Chucai were chatting in their tent, a soldier rushed in and reported: "The old monk hasn't gone to bed yet. He is holding a stone jar and praying with tears in his eyes. We don't know why." Yelü Chucai smiled, then said, "You've done well to keep a close watch on him, but don't disturb him. Report immediately if you notice anything new." After the soldier had left, Genghis Khan and Yelü Chucai went to sleep, but before long there came a thunderous explosion with golden rays dancing in all directions, and outside the tents was total confusion. The soldier ran up to report breathlessly that at the fifth watch the old monk had walked out of the temple with the stone jar held tightly in his arms. Soldiers had run up to stop him, but the old monk had been so powerful that dozens could not halt him. He had run to a cliff and leapt off it. With a thunderous explosion he had dropped to the ground at the foot of the cliff and disappeared, and at the place had appeared a spring of water.

Genghis Khan and Yelü Chucai dressed quickly and went to the spot to look; the flat land had become a vast area of billowing water. Very pleased, Genghis Khan ordered a palace to be built at the place and the lake to be named Jar Hill Pond.

Yelü Chucai had known that Jar Hill was a hill of gold,

the stone jar was a treasure and the old monk was the incarnation of the God of Wealth. He had wanted to curry favour with Genghis Khan by presenting these treasures to him but had not expected the old monk to outwit him by turning the treasure into a stream of water.

On his deathbed Yelü Chucai said to Emperor Taizong of the Yuan, successor to Genghis Khan, "I have one thing to beg Your Majesty: please bury me beside Jar Hill Pond when I die, firstly because I like the beautiful scenery there and secondly because there are many treasures in the lake which need somebody to keep guard. I want to serve Your Majesty even after I die." The Emperor Taizong did as he was begged. Many years later, when the Emperor Qianlong of the Qing Dynasty dug Jar Hill Pond into Kunming Lake, Yelü Chucai's tomb was removed to the small courtyard of the present-day Tower of Perceiving the Spring. The stone stele was erected by Qianlong at that time.

How the Seventeen-Arch Bridge Was Built

THE Seventeen-Arch Bridge, the biggest bridge in the Summer Palace, is 150 metres long, connecting the Octagonal Tower in the east and the South Lake Isle in the south. With white marble balustrades carved with lions, the bridge looks like a rainbow linking the human world with the Penglai Fairyland.

Tradition has it that when the Seventeen-Arch Bridge was built during the Qianlong Reign of the Qing Dynasty, many skilful craftsmen were employed to quarry the blocks of white marble from the mountains in Fangshan County. One day an old man of seventy or eighty came to the building site, his long, dishevelled hair hanging down to his ears, his face covered with dust and a toolbox on his back. He walked along hawking his wares: "A Dragon-door Stone! Who wants to buy it?" Seeing the filth on him, the people took him for a madman, and no one paid him any attention. He roamed about the worksite for three days without arousing any notice.

The old man left the worksite and walked east. When he

reached Liulang Village he halted under a big scholartree. At night he slept in the open under the tree, and at cockcrow he rose to chisel his big Dragon-door Stone with an iron hammer. One evening it began to rain very hard, and he took shelter squatting under the tree with his arms over his head. At this moment Grandpa Wang from the western end of the village passed by. He took pity on the old man and asked him into his house.

With a place to live and food to eat, the old man stayed at Grandpa Wang's home for a whole year, working on his stone day by day. One morning he said to Grandpa Wang, "I'll be leaving today. I've lived on you for a whole year and will never forget your kindness. I have nothing to repay you with except this stone." Grandpa Wang cast a glance at the stone and said, "Don't say that. As for the stone, you've worked hard on it for a whole year. You'd better take it away with you. I don't need it." "It will fetch more than one hundred taels of silver when it's sold at the right moment," the old man said, then left for the south.

When the Seventeen-Arch Bridge was nearly complete, word came that the Emperor Qianlong would come in person to celebrate the completion of the project, but unexpectedly the last stone which was to be put in the middle of the bridge could not be chiselled no matter how great an effort was made. This so worried the chief engineer of the project that he was reminded of the old man trying to sell the Dragon-door Stone and immediately sent people to search for him.

On learning that the old mason had lived in Liulang Village, the chief engineer went to find him at Grandpa Wang's place, and as soon as he reached there, he spotted the stone lying beside a window. He went to measure it, and to his surprise, it was exactly the size he wanted, as if it had been made specially for the bridge. Happy beyond words, he said to Grandpa Wang, "This stone was made by a god from heaven specially for the bridge. It will save me. How much will you take for it?" "I don' t want too much," Grandpa Wang said. "The old mason stayed at my place for a whole year and didn't pay me for his food. You just give me the cost of that." The chief engineer gave him a hundred taels of silver and took the stone away.

The stone fitted into place perfectly on the bridge, and so the project was finally completed. All the builders heaved a sigh of relief: "If we hadn't completed the bridge, the Emperor would have killed us for it." As they rejoiced over their success, it suddenly dawned on an old builder, who said, "Fellow masters, it must have been Lu Ban who came to help us build the bridge!"

The story about Lu Ban helping to build the Seventeen-Arch Bridge has been told far and wide ever since.

The Mother and Son Rocks

IN front of the Hall of Jade Billows in the Summer Palace stand two rocks. Tradition has it that one is male and the Emperor Guangxu and the other is female and his mother the Empress Dowager Cixi. They face each other stoically day and night and have come to be known as "The Mother and Son Rocks".

After the Reform Movement of 1898 failed, the Empress Dowager Cixi had her son, the Emperor Guangxu, confined to Yingtai in Nanhai near the Forbidden City. One day the Empress Dowager wanted to go to the Summer Palace but could not leave Guangxu and his favourite concubine Zhenfei alone in the city, so she decided to take them along with her, without letting them meet each other.

Upon arrival in the Summer Palace, the Emperor was confined in the Hall of Jade Billows. He felt very grieved. All birds, flowers and the skies outside the hall seemed to him to be weeping. At a time like this he missed all the more his concubine Zhenfei, who had gone through thick and thin together with him during the Reform Movement, but he could not tell anybody what was on his mind.

His personal eunuch Wang Shang understood him. One night, when the Empress Dowager had gone to bed, Wang Shang bribed the maid who guarded Zhenfei and spirited the concubine to the Emperor. When they met, they had a lot to tell each other and hated to part again. They talked and wept until the moon hung overhead.

Suddenly a young eunuch's cough was heard; this was a signal that either the Empress Dowager herself or one of her lackeys was coming. What was to be done? It was too late for Zhenfei to go back. If the Empress Dowager found her there, not only would the Emperor and his concubine suffer greatly, but also the eunuch Wang Shang and others would be beheaded. The Emperor shook with fear. "It doesn't matter if I die," Zhenfei said to Wang Shang with tears, "but I'm sorry to have involved you all."

"Don't worry, Your Majesty," Wang Shang said quickly, "I've got an idea." He walked to a full-length mirror in the southeastern corner of the hall and turned the knob on it. A wardrobe opened big enough for a person to hide in. Zhenfei went in.

A moment later, escorted by the chief eunuch Li Lianying, the Empress Dowager arrived with a crowd of maids. What had happened was that eunuch had discovered a light still burning in the hall late at night and become suspicious. He had gone to find out what was going on there but been stopped by the Emperor's man, who had said the Emperor was reading and no one should disturb him. The eunuch had reported this to the Empress Dowager, who, suspicious and heartless as she was, had come to have a look herself.

The Emperor Guangxu hastily knelt to greet his mother. The Empress Dowager seated herself slowly, looked around and saw nothing suspicious in the hall. Then she said hypocritically, "You must pay attention to your health. Don't work too hard." The Emperor was too desperately worried that his concubine would be spotted to hear what she said. He just kept nodding his head and saying, "Yes, yes." The Empress Dowager was enraged and pointing to the rock on the left in front of the hall, shouted: "You are as heartless as the rock over there!" Her cry startled the Emperor, who promptly dropped to his knees, saying, "Yes, yes, I am a rock!" The Empress Dowager gave him a ferocious stare and left.

When she was gone, the Emperor leant against the gate of the hall and said to the rock on the right, "She has a heart colder than that rock!"

After that the eunuchs and maids of the Summer Palace called the two rocks "The Mother and Son Rocks", and today they still have the same names.

The Marble Boat

IN the Summer Palace there also lies a two-storey Marble Boat carved out of one whole block. To its east are the Hall for Listening to the Orioles and the Hundred-League Tower, and to its south is the vast Kunming Lake.

To celebrate her fiftieth birthday the Empress Dowager Cixi issued an order to build a longevity park. She asked one of her personal eunuchs to make the preparations. The eunuch knew it was an enormous project which needed a lot of money. Where was he to get it? He went to consult the Empress Dowager.

"Go to the minister of defence," said the Empress Dowager.

The eunuch was puzzled. The building of the park was the work of the ministry of internal affairs: why should she tell him to go to the minister of defence? However, he had to do what he was told.

Who was the minister of defence? He was the Emperor Guangxu's father, who was a prince. His four-year-old son had been chosen as successor to the throne and become emperor after the old Emperor Tongzhi died, and he himself had been promoted from being an ordinary prince to the powerful ministry of defence. To curry favour with the Empress Dowager, he had built three imperial parks, the Qianhai, Zhonghai and Houhai, and established a department to handle naval affairs immediately after he had assumed office.

When the eunuch went to him, he understood immediately that the Empress Dowager wanted to divert the funds earmarked for the navy. But to do so, he must find an excuse. He wagged his head, and an idea sprang to his mind. "Ah!" he said to himself, "I'll say I'm using the money to train the navy."

Under this pretext he began to use the naval funds. The Empress Dowager was very pleased and increased the naval funds by another one million taels of silver in addition to allowing him to draw on the Coastal Defence and Customs Tax.

The construction of the park was a big project. Magnificent buildings were set up both on the hill and below it. When the project was completed they called the place a naval school and had some recruits trained on Kunming Lake.

When it was time to celebrate the birthday of the Empress Dowager the whole park was decorated with lanterns and coloured streamers, drums boomed and gongs sounded, and all high civil and military officers came to offer their congratulations. Very pleased, the Empress Dowager richly rewarded the navy before she took the officials round the park.

When the procession reached the western end of the Long

Corridor and passed through the Hall for Listening to the Orioles and the Hundred-League Tower they came upon a huge stone warship with awesome stone cannons on it. The cannons' mouths were turned on Longevity Hill. The Empress Dowager became very angry at the sight of this. "Why did they construct such a monster here?" she shouted. "Take it away at once!"

"Don' t be angry, Your Majesty," the eunuch said quickly. "We can't do without the boat. Otherwise what will we say about the naval funds?"

"Don't worry, Your Majesty," the minister of defence put in. "This is only a model."

The Empress Dowager knew it well at heart, but she still thought that it did not look pleasant to have a stone warship in the beautiful park, so she said instead, "Take those stone cannons away then."

All the high officials knew that the Empress Dowager wanted a carved marble boat there, where she could drink and seek pleasure. They dismantled the stone cannons and built a marble boat there instead.

The Empress Dowager was very pleased. Later she expelled the naval school from the park and made the place a forbidden imperial park.

The Dragon King Temple and Golden Hook River

ON South Lake Isle in Kunming Lake stands the Dragon King Temple. Why was the temple built on the tiny isle in the lake?

In ancient times Longevity Hill was called Jar Hill, and the small lake before it was called Jar Hill Pond. The dike on the eastern bank of the lake was called the Western Dike. Around Jar Hill lay numerous springs, which provided water for the nearby villagers to drink, irrigate their fields and raise ducks, fish and crabs.

In a certain ancient dynasty it had not rained in three years, there was no water coming from the springs, Jar Hill Pond almost became dry, and rice in the fields began to wither. People flowed to the Western Dike to kneel down together, burning incense and kowtowing to beg the God of Heaven for rain. But the God of Heaven seemed to set itself against them. It was already past June 13, but not one drop of rain was seen.

One day a white-bearded old man came to the Western

Dike and told the people that he could raise the water of Jar Hill Pond by three inches a night and one foot a day, and once the pond was filled up there would be no fear of drought even if it didn't rain for another three years. When asked how he could do that, he explained: "Several thousand years ago the place was a sea. The sea water receded and left a marsh with ponds. There is a sea well at the bottom of the pond near the Western Dike. The reason why the pond is drying up is because a goldfish demon has blocked the sea well. If the goldfish demon is removed, the water will come up."

The villagers pleaded with the white-bearded old man for help to find the goldfish demon.

The old man asked them to jump into the pond together with him. After walking a few times round the sandy beach, he stopped at a place and made a cross with his boot on the ground and said, "Dig down three feet here, and you will find the sea well."

The villagers did as they were told, and when they had dug down three feet, sure enough the mouth of a spring was found, where a goldfish with a golden head, tail and scales lay still in the muddy water. "We've found the goldfish demon!" cried the villagers as they ran away to spread the news.

Just at this moment the goldfish made a sudden leap, and water welled up and was very soon up to the dike.

In gratitude the villagers turned to look at the white-bearded old man, but he was nowhere to be seen. Some people said it must have been the Dragon King who had materialized to deliver water for them, so the villagers donated money and materials and built a temple on the Western Dike to the Dragon King. Every year from April 1 to 15 all the people from the nearby villages came there to beg the Dragon King for protection.

During the reign of Qianlong of the Qing the Western Dike was taken down, the lake bank extended to the east, Jar Hill Pond was renamed Kunming Lake, and the Dragon King Temple became an isle in the lake.

Where had the little goldfish gone? It was said that it had swum west and disappeared into Yangshui Lake, where every midnight golden light glistened on the water. When a eunuch named Cao learned the news, he decided to get hold of the goldfish and ordered his men to dig in the lake to find it. They dug for three days but found no trace. Then at midnight the golden light appeared in the south. The next day Eunuch Cao ordered his men to dig in the direction of the golden light, but they failed again. This continued until they reached the city of Beijing. Still they did not find the goldfish. However, the ditch they dug became a river and led the water of Jade Spring Hill and Jar Hill Pond to the city. The river later became known as Golden Hook River or Golden River. The end of their digging in the city became a pond called Goldfish Pond.

Beihai Park

BEIHAI Park, situated northwest of the Imperial Palace and Jingshan Park, is a large imperial garden with a long history. Its construction started as early as the Liao and Jin dynasties eight hundred years ago. The succeeding Yuan Dynasty built its capital Dadu around the park, which became the foundation of the inner city of present-day Beijing. Expansion was carried out in the Ming and Qing dynasties, though it remained a private imperial garden. The layout of Beihai Park manifests the tradition of China's ancient gardens. In the south of its waters is Qionghua Islet with pavilions and halls built along the bank. The islet consists of structures such as the White Dagoba, Hall of Ripples, Pavilion for Inspecting Old Script and Happy Heart Hall. The main buildings along the bank are the Five Dragon Pavilions, Nine Dragon Screen Wall, Iron Screen, Hall of the Heavenly King, Tranquil Heart Study and Moat Pool. To the west of the south gate of Beihai is the Round City with the Hall of Received Light sitting in the middle. In 1925 Beihai became a public park. Since Liberation it has been thoroughly renovated and is now a famous scenic spot of the capital.

Iron Screen

ON the north bank of Beihai, to the northeast of the Five Dragon Pavilions, is an outstanding screen coloured dark red and looking as if it is made of iron, called the Iron Screen. As a matter of fact, it was not made of iron but a volcanic mineral. The Iron Screen was moved here in 1946 from Fruit Market Street inside the Gate of Moral Victory. Five hundred years ago, it was not there either but stood before a temple outside the Gate of Moral Victory. Why was it moved to Fruit Market Street? A legend tells the story.

Many many years ago there were two dragons in Youzhou, one male, the other female. When city walls were built around Beijing, they took the form of an old man and wife and led a leisurely life in a secluded place. Yet they found the northwest wind added several inches of sand to Beijing each time it blew, which it did for three to four days. Both the old man and his wife were concerned, saying, "If this goes on, Beijing will soon be submerged."

"Something is behind this," said the old woman.

"I agree with you," said the old man.

"But what could it be?"

They worried for many days without a solution. And the wind went on blowing fiercely.

One day, when crossing a bridge at the Front Gate, an old man and the long-eared grey donkey he was tiding were blown up to the sky by a sudden northwesterly gust. In fright, the donkey pricked up its ears, and the old man closed his eyes. Soon the wind abated, and the donkey touched ground. On opening his eyes, the old man found himself outside the Gate of Exalted Literature. He had flown in the air for almost two miles. Another day, a young monk in Huanggu Temple in the Western Hills was borne up in the air by a gale when playing outside the temple. He was so frightened that he wrapped his arms around his head, shut his eyes and, with a thumping heart, thought: "I'll doubtless fall to my death." Soon the wind abated, and his feet touched ground. On opening his eyes, he saw that he was in the city of Beijing. He had flown in the air for a long distance.

It was an odd wind, indeed. The old man and woman who had been dragons were even more concerned on hearing the above incidents. One day the old man said to his wife, "Let's take a stroll and see if we can find out something." The old woman answered: "Quite right, we can' t find out a thing by sitting here." So the old couple emerged from their home. Where should they go? Since the wind had come from the northwest, they followed that direction and saw on their way pedlars,

customers, carriers — all ordinary people in ordinary clothes talking and doing ordinary things. They saw no odd people or happenings. They walked on and on until they came to the northwest corner of the city. The old woman began to complain: "You just followed your whim and headed in any direction you liked. We' ve come to the corner of the city without seeing anything. We ought to take a look outside the city."

The old man laughed. "Don't grumble. We can turn east and go out of the north gate."

As soon as the old couple turned east they saw something odd. Sitting beside the wall were two people — an old woman in her fifties and a boy in his teens, both clad in clothes the colour of dirt and both covered with dust from head to toe and as ugly as could be. Each was holding a dirt-coloured bag. The old woman was filling her bag with sand and the boy his with cotton as they chatted. Being too far away to hear clearly, all the old man and woman could hear was, "We'll certainly bury the city of Beijing."

The dragon man looked at his wife, who nodded to him knowingly. These two must be Granny Wind and Cloud Boy making plans to engulf Beijing. At the sight of the approaching couple they straightened up. Granny Wind told Cloud Boy, "Let's go home, grandson. Your mother is waiting for you."

To stop them from escaping, the old man shot forward to block Granny Wind's way, while his wife stopped Cloud Boy. Pointing at Granny Wind, the old man demanded: "Whatever are you trying to do? There're a large number of people living in Beijing. Why do you scheme to bury the city?"

Granny Wind gave a cold laugh: "How dare you interfere with me, you old codger? The city blocked my route when it was built. Of course I want to bury it."

The old man broke into a peal of laughter and then said, "How dare an old biddy like you do that? Give up your bag of sand right now." Then he pointed at Cloud Boy: "You must hand over your bag of rotten cotton too. You ought to learn to be good at your age."

Cloud Boy didn't even wait for Granny Wind to open her mouth before he tipped his bag up and poured out a stream of black clouds, shouting at the same time, "Granny, pour out the wind and sand."

The dragon man and woman opened their mouths and inhaled, swallowing duster after duster of black clouds. When they had barely swallowed all the clouds, wind and sand rolled up, choking them. Atishoo! The old man sneezed. Atishoo! So did the old woman. Their sneezes sent four spurts of water straight at Granny Wind and Cloud Boy. Exclaiming in dismay, Granny Wind grabbed Cloud Boy's hand and flew up to the sky. The old man and woman, resuming dragon form, followed in hot pursuit. Since that time, the city of Beijing has had less wind and sand. People give the credit to Grandpa Dragon and Grandma Dragon, who drove away Granny Wind and Cloud Boy. They say: "Since Granny Wind and Cloud Boy fear Grandpa and Grandma Dragon, let's forge an iron screen with a dragon on each side to keep them away." So we have a majestic iron screen in Beijing.

Many many years later the northern wall of the city was pulled down and moved further south, exposing the former north city to wind and sand. The Beijing inhabitants were worried, not knowing what to do. A knowledgeable old gentleman said, "Now that we are too far from the Iron Screen, Grandpa Dragon and Grandma Dragon can't protect us against Granny Wind and Cloud Boy. We should do something about it." All those who knew the story behind the Iron Screen agreed with him. But what could they do? A clever man said, "Set your minds at ease, my fellow citizens. I have an idea." What was his idea? He proposed to have the Iron Screen moved into the city. It was certainly a "clever idea". So the Iron Screen was moved to stand outside a temple on Fruit Market Street. Later this street was renamed Iron Screen Lane.

Golden Buns

"**O**NE in danger is grateful to his benefactor,

One in adversity is easily contented,

One in luck becomes arrogant and spoilt,

One in power throws his weight about."

The above saying has been circulating among the Chinese people from generation to generation, the truth of it attested by the story of the Empress Dowager Cixi eating golden buns.

Fangshan Restaurant in Beihai Park was originally the imperial kitchen of the Qing-dynasty Emperor and the Empress Dowager. To this day it still serves tiny *wowotou* (corn buns) made of a mashed chestnuts the size of an almond. People buy them in pastry boxes out of curiosity as well as to eat or as gifts, as these are said to be the golden buns the Empress Dowager fancied. How was it that *wowotou*, a food of the poor, was included in the imperial cuisine? It concerns an adventure of the Empress Dowager.

Cixi lived an extravagant life when she bacame the Empress Dowager. Hundreds of chefs cooked hundreds of dishes for her in the imperial kitchen day and night. Food had to be delivered the minute she ordered it and done just right, the right temperature, tenderness, crispness, colour and taste, and no two dishes might be similar. Her daily menu included a long list of dishes. But of all these delicacies from land and sea she took only an occasional mouthful, sometimes barely touched them with her chopsticks or waved them away with a mere glance. She was so choosy that few of the hundreds of thousands of meals were palatable to her, so much so that her cuisine became a special branch of learning. At court there emerged people who were nothing but expert caters and drinkers, who accompanied her when she visited scenic spots and held banquets. Wherever they went they sought out special local products and had them prepared in many ways.

Such was the way she lived until to the rumble of gunfire the Allied Forces of the Eight Powers attacked the city of Beijing. The imperial palace was in turmoil, and the terrified Empress Dowager fled with the Emperor and his court ladies. Disguised as a poor peasant woman, the Empress Dowager fled helter-skelter out of Xizhimen Gate in a blue cloth dress and black cloth shoes, on an ordinary cart pulled by mules and went secretly to the Summer Palace, where she ordered her ministers to transport her jewelry to Jehol and the eunuchs to prepare food for her to eat on the way. But the sound of gunshots intensified as the Allied Forces advanced. It was so deafening and scaring that the Empress Dowager crawled

on to the mule cart and left the Summer Palace in a hurry leaving her jewelry behind.

The Empress Dowager fled to Shanxi nonstop on the iron-wheeled cart, which tossed her violently on the bumpy road. The weather was rainy, and she was cold and hungry and anxious too. As darkness fell she saw cooking smoke rising from a thatched hut at the foot of a mountain. She told the cart to stop so that she could get out of the rain and cold and get something to eat. They could start again after a rest. They alighted and entered the hut, which had a brick bed half covered with a straw mat. On it were a sewing basket and a thin coverlet under a pillow filled with straw. Bent before the stove beside the brick bed was an old woman feeding the fire. Looking up, she mistook the Empress Dowager for some passerby coming in to shelter from the rain. She greeted her warmly: "It's hard to be on the road in the cold rain and wind. Please get on to the warm brick bed."

The Empress Dowager flopped down on the bed feeling like a piece of chewed string. Not wanting to expose her identity, she feigned amicability as she told her: "I haven't had anything to drink or eat since morning. What are you cooking on the stove?"

The old woman lifted the pot lid and handed the Empress Dowager a steaming *wowotou*, saying warmly, "This is a *wowotou*. Eat it while it's hot."

Her hands quivering and her stomach rumbling from hunger, the Empress Dowager accepted the *wowotou* and took a bite. It was soft and spongy and warmed her stomach, making her comfortable and relaxed. She ate three at one go and still wanted more. She couldn't help saying, "This golden bun is so delicious. What is it made of?"

The old woman answered: "Poor as I am, I don't have anything good. It is nothing but ground corn made into a hollowed conical bun. It is our staple food all the year round." The peasants have such good staple food all the year round, thought the Empress Dowager, while I have never even set eyes on it. So they have been keeping good things from me. I'll give them a piece of my mind when we return to the palace. She felt grateful to have this warm brick bed and good food in peril and wanted to thank this scrawny old woman. What could she give her when she didn' t have any of her silver and gold, silk and jewelry with her? As she smoothed her hair, she touched a gold hairpin, which she put at the edge of the bed and told the old woman: "I'll never forget your kindness all my life. This gold hairpin is a reward for your kindness."

The old woman looked at her and then at the hairpin without a word.

"Take it. This is a reward for your three buns. It's a good bargain for you."

The old woman shook her head, placed the gold hairpin in the Empress Dowager' s hand and smiled. "We poor people are used to hardship, and we're not greedy. This is precious. You had better keep it. Although I'm hard up, I would not turn a passer-by in difficulty away. I want no silver or gold.

But if you trust me, tell me who you are."

The Empress Dowager's face fell. She wants to know who I am. Does she want my life? Is there anyone who prefers truth to gold? She must have evil motives. I must take to my heels. Sticking the hairpin in her hair, she took her leave, saying, "I am a person in peril. If my luck should turn, I'll show my gratitude for your saving my life." She walked out of the hut immediately. The carter quickly hopped down to help her as she climbed on to the cart. The old woman stood at the door to see her off, but the Empress Dowager never once turned back.

Li Hongzhang negotiated with the Allied Forces, signed the traitorous Treaty of Shimonoseki and wantonly slaughtered the Yihequan (the Boxers). The Empress Dowager brought disgrace on the country and sacrificed hundreds and thousands of lives for her own safety. Amid gongs and drums and surrounded by her retinue she returned in state to Beijing, where she held court for her ministers, threw banquets, admired flowers, went boating and watched operas and lantern shows. Again she lived in extravagance and enjoyed herself as if nothing had happened. Her kitchen slaughtered chickens and geese and was busy cooking all day long. Yet she never liked the food, taking a bite and pulling a long face as she frowned at a table laden with food. Her court ladies and chefs were worried and scared, asking her dozens of times a day, "What would you like to eat, Old Buddha?"

She sighed. "All my life I've had only one good meal. It

was golden hollowed conical buns made of corn, so soft and spongy, and they warmed my stomach. Alas that an empress dowager does not have as good food as ordinary people!"

No one in the palace had ever seen or eaten golden corn buns. No one knew their taste. No one knew how to make the *wowotou* the Empress Dowager fancied. One young man, a helper in the kitchin, a clever and brave young man, racked his brains until the truth came home to him: when one's full nothing tastes good; when one's hungry everything is honey. When the Empress Dowager was taking flight, having nothing to eat, she would find a corn bun delicious in her hunger. Now that she is back in the palace, how could she swallow such coarse food? He formed a plan and volunteered, "I' ll make golden buns for the Empress Dowager."

Everyone was worried for him. Gleefully the young man told them: "A monk living deep in the mountains gave me some golden corn which gives the eater long life. I' ll make golden buns for the Empress Dowager. But the monk told me that before eating this golden bun one must abstain from food and meditate for a whole day. Then this golden bun will give long life."

The Empress Dowager was delighted when she heard this and ordered the eunuchs to prepare a place for her to meditate with no one to disturb her.

Unhurriedly the young man roasted chestnuts, ground them into powder, mixed it with cassia, lotus-root powder, eggs and a little cornflour. He made the mixture into tiny hollowed conical buns the size of an almond. When he steamed them they smelled delicious. When they were brought to the Empress Dowager, who had had no food for a whole day, she picked up one and took a bite. It was soft and spongy, sweet and fragrant. Her face wreathed in smiles, she turned and said, "This is what I ate when I was fleeing from danger. This is the staple food of the ordinary people. Who says they have a hard life? The golden buns the peasants eat are much bigger than mine."

Zhongshan Park

ZHONGSHAN Park, located to the southwest of the Imperial Palace, was originally the site of the Altar of Land and Grain in the Ming and Qing dynasties. In 1914 it was opened as a public park, and as Sun Yat-sen's coffin had rested in it in 1925, it was renamed Zhongshan Park in 1928 in memory of him after an adopted alias.

Its main buildings are the Altar of Land and Grain, the Homage Hall and the Greenhouse, the Pavilion of the Orchid Pavilion Steles, the Water Pavilion, the Concert Hall and the Memorial Gateway.

The Descent of the Gods of Farming

PAYING homage to the gods of Land and Grain was the grandest ceremony of the emperors and princes. A slate and a long block of wood on the altar symbolize She, the god of land, and Ji, the god of grain.

At the ceremony, the places of these gods were taken by two "tillers". In the seat of She was a geographer and pedologist expert in distinguishing the soil and how to plant various crops. He was honoured as God of Land. In the seat of Ji was a god named Qi (usually called Ji), an "agronomist", born it was said, when his mother on a chance excursion into the suburbs became pregnant as she tried to fit her foot into a big footprint on the ground. Fatherless, the baby was deserted, but the beasts fed and protected him. Later people took him home and named him Qi, meaning "the deserted". Qi loved planting, and whenever he played he put wild seeds in the earth. When the plants ripened, they were much bigger and sweeter than wild ones. He taught people how to plant, and they had all they needed. He exhorted them to farm and become wealthy. Today, on Mount Jiwang in Wenxi County, Shanxi Province, there remain coloured stones, some of which look like ears of wheat, others like green beans. They were said to have come from the seeds left by Qi. People call them "Grain Stones".

The Altar of Land and Grain in the capital was called Imperial She and Ji, while those in the prefectures were She and Ji. Each year, the Emperor held a great ceremony in the capital, while local officials conducted lesser ceremonies in other parts of the country.

Zhongnanhai

LOCATED west of the Forbidden City and south of Beihai Park, Zhongnanhai consists of two parts, Zhonghai and Nanhai, the former built in the Jin Dynasty and the latter in the Ming. It was then called, together with the present-day Beihai Park, Xihaizi or Taiyechi. It was divided into Zhongnanhai and Beihai in the early years of the Republic, when the Treasure Moon Mansion, now called the Xinhua Gate, on the southern bank of Nanhai Lake was renovated.

On the eastern bank of Nanhai Lake stand mansions and pavilions named the Gurgling Waters, the Thousand Feet of Snow, the Intimate Reeds, the Raindrops and Banana Tree and the Cloud Cap. Nanhai also includes the Qinzheng Hall and Yingtai Island, on which the Emperor Guangxu was imprisoned by the Empress Dowager Cixi during the late Qing Dynasty. Zhonghai includes the halls and pavilions of the Blossom, the Lively Pool, the Bumper Harvest, the Benevolent Dwelling and the Purple Light.

Home Mansion

IN the Qianlong Period of the Qing Dynasty there lived in the northwest of the country a beautiful Uygur girl whose body produced a mysterious fragrance, and people called her Fragrant Maiden.

When the Emperor Qianlong heard about this he had her brought to Beijing, the capital.

When she arrived the Emperor kept her under close watch and sent his men to persuade her to be his concubine. But Fragrant Maiden rejected him. There was nothing he could do about it.

For years she was cooped up in the heavily guarded imperial garden and she became homesick, though she had wonderful food, lived in glamorous mansions and wore gold and jade. Most Uygurs were Muslims. To please Fragrant Maiden, the Emperor Qianlong allowed her Islamic food and living arrangements, but this did not help either. Then he had another idea: he had a grand mosque built just opposite Treasure Moon Mansion like those in her homeland, a two-storeyed building about ten metres high, behind which lived her fellow Uygurs who had come to Beijing with her. At that time there were two main sects of Muslims, one group wearing blue cotton caps and the other wearing white cotton caps, but those who had come with Fragrant Maiden wore red cotton caps.

Every time she grew homesick, the Emperor would send for the court ladies to accompany her to Treasure Moon Mansion, from the balcony of which she would look south to the mosque, which reminded her of her red-capped fellow nationals, made her feel at home and comforted her. Fences both on the eastern and western sides of the mosque kept out strangers.

Home Mansion is gone, and so are the fences. Treasure Moon Mansion has been renamed Xinhua Gate, but there is still a Double Fence Lane off Western Chang'an Boulevard, where many Muslim families still live.

The tale of Fragrant Maiden has passed down from generation to generation of Beijingers.

The Fragrant Hills

THE Fragrant Hills, a quiet scenic spot in the western suburbs of Beijing, are famous for their undulating, flowered and wooded ranges and places of historical interest. Already in the Liao Dynasty (907-1125) private villas ware built there; in the Jin, Yuan, Ming and Qing dynasties, pleasure palaces were constructed for the imperial families. In the tenth and eleventh years of the Qianlong Reign of the Qing Dynasty, a large-scale addition took place, making the Fragrant Hills a complex of twenty-eight scenic locales, renamed the Park of Tranquillity and Pleasure. The magnificent five-storeyed Fragrant Hill Temple, built in the Jin Dynasty, is the most important of the many there. The Twin Pool Villa, where Mao Zedong and the Central Committee of the Communist Party lived in March, 1949 during the War of Liberation, has become a memorial to the victory of the Chinese revolution. Besides these, the Pavilion of Revealing One's Mind, the precipitous Devil's Awe Cliff, the five hundred arhats with various expressions in the Biyun Temple and the limpid streams in Cherry Gully are focuses of tourist attraction. The natural vista of the Fragrant Hills red leaves, redolent of flame, on which countless poems have been witten, has become the most picturesque spot.

The Fragrant Hills and the Treasure Crock

WHY are the Fragrant Hills so wooded? The legend tells that in ancient times there was a well-known skilful stonemason named Old Zhang in the Western Hills, who chiselled almost all the millstones, solid and reliable, for the nearby villagers. One year, Landlord Zhao Delu, living up the hill, asked him to chisel a pig trough. Old Zhang said it was easy and in no time made a huge rock on the roadside into a trough.

Zhao Delu hired a labourer, Wang Shusheng, the youngest son of the Wang Family at the foot of the hill. The first time Wang Shusheng used the trough to feed pigs, he found it was a treasure crock, for half a bucket of pigswill still remained after three pigs had eaten their fill. Wang kept it for himself.

At the end of the year it was time to draw his wages. "Master," said Wang to Zhao, "my family has been in need of a pig trough, and I wonder if you would let me have your trough as my wages." Unaware of the ins and outs of the matter, Zhao thought he could take advantage of it. How many troughs a year's wages would have bought! Laughing inwardly at Wang's foolishness, Zhao complimented him hypocritically: "You're a good farmer. Take what you wish! Tomorrow I'll tell Old Zhang to chisel me another one." Fearing that Wang might go back on his words, he urged him to take it home immediately.

Long journeys are tiresome. Half way up the hill, Shusheng felt the weight of the hundred *jin* trough on his shoulder and stopped on a slope to rest. Suddenly a strong gust of wind blew up the sand and stones, and the sky darkened. Shusheng pondered: I simply can't get it home in such treacherous weather. I'd better bury it here until the weather turns good. With this in mind, he started digging and covering, then stuck a pine seedling in the mound as a mark and went home. The wind kept blowing, and the sky became clear after the Spring Festival. With ropes Shusheng went into the mountains to fetch the trough. Stopping half way down the hill, he was dumbfounded to see no sign of the pine seedling and that the whole hill was covered with arm-thick pines which spread in all directions from where he had buried the trough. The seedling had grown into a pine forest in a few days after it was stuck into the treasure crock.

Later people claimed that the trough rock was a celestial stone, the remains of the stones which Nüwa had used to mend the sky.* Because the rock looked like an incense

---

* Nüwa is supposed to have made human beings out of mud, melted five-coloured stones to mend the sky, broken off the legs of a turtle to support the four poles, brought floods under control and killed fierce beasts so as to give people a stable life.

burner, the hill was called Incense-burner Peak, soon contracted to Fragrant Hill. And the tallest sturdy pine on the hill, which is supposed to be the original seedling, became the Tree King. Later a temple was erected behind the Tree King and called Fragrant Hill Temple. The pine stretched its branches towards the gate of the temple as if it was listening to the monks preaching, thus earning the name of the Listening Pine.

The Fragrant Hills' Red Leaves

ONCE upon a time, at the foot of the Fragrant Hills lived a sixty-year-old man Yuqing and his daughter Chuanhong, who kept each other's company for survival. Every day the old man went into the hills to collect mushrooms, while the daughter stayed at home weaving cloth. Her delicate hands wove wildflowers into the cloth, as fresh as if they were just picked from the hills.

"Dad!" said the daughter happily one day. "I hear there are five-coloured clouds on top of the Fragrant Hills. I want to have a look at them and then weave them into cloth."

"That sounds good. But you shouldn't run about!"

The next day, Yuqing took his daughter into the hills. Chuanhong, like a freed deer, picked flowers and grass here and there the whole way. She was simply beside herself with joy! When they were half way up the Fragrant Hills, the daughter said she was too thirsty to continue.

"Wait a few minutes, child!" said the old man. "As soon as we get to the top of the hill, I'll dig up some Bitter Dew grass on the north side to quench your thirst."

Bushy and woody, steep and perilous, the gully was the lair of a huge black serpent which had stealthily eaten the thousand-year-old glossy ganoderma and could change into human form after years of eating wind and dew, committing all kinds of outrages. One day when it was sunning itself on a big flat rock, a girl as beautiful as a celestial suddenly came into its view, picking flowers. A wicked idea occurred to it, but on seeing the old herb-collector following behind, it changed its mind. It had once almost been caught by him, and had escaped with only the loss of an inch of its tail! It wanted to change into human form but was afraid that this ruse would be seen through. At a complete loss what to do, it heard the girl saying she was thirsty. It pulled a few red pearls from its head and threw them out. They immediately turned into a bunch of red mountain apricots. White touched with red, they were like a pool of crystal-clear water. In those days the Fragrant Hills didn't have any red leaves but were covered with these mountain apricot trees. In spring the blossoms, white as snow, were called Clear Snow of the Western Hills; in summer the trees were heavy with fruit whose fragrance wafted ten miles away. Now it was almost autumn, so why were there apricots in the mountain still? Happy and surprised at her discovery, Chuanhong shouted out, "Daddy! Hurry and look! Here is a bunch of ripe red apricots!"

Yuqing came up and examined them carefully, and he was confused too. Sniffing, he found they really were late apricots and picked them for his daughter.

Taking them, she ran to a huge rock and sat down to eat. Just as she had finished one apricot and her father had blown a puff of smoke, the remaining apricots on the twig suddenly began to drop and turned out to be snake eggs!

Yuqing was stunned and lost his composure: "Damn it! We are beset by an evil spirit. Let's go!" By now his daughter's face was crimson and her lips looked as if she had just put on rouge.

The old man hastily poured out all the collected herbs. Finding the sweet licorice and the antidotal grass, the old man said, "Be quick! Put these in your mouth and chew!" With these words, he grasped her hand and started to run. After only a few steps she fell to the ground. The old man shouted her name, but no matter how hard he did so, she remained unconscious, with her eyes tight closed and her face turning purple. Yuqing moved her on to a flat rock, then hurried downhill to look for spring water and an antidote.

The serpent came out from behind the rock. Finding the girl lying on the roadside, it immediately bore down on her, but was nearly choked to death by the circle of tobacco set by the old man. With hatred of the old man in its heart, the serpent also hurried downhill and turned itself into a temple with the Great Goddess of the Ninth Heaven in it. Running forward, the old man was startled to see a small temple at the foot of the hill. Perhaps too anxious to seek a doctor, the old man entered the temple without giving it a second thought. Kneeling down and kowtowing, he pleaded, "Your Majesty, Goddess of the Ninth Heaven, I don't know what celestials I have offended to make my daughter suffer like this. I beg Your Majesty to have mercy on me and save my daughter's life, and I'll burn incense and offer sacrifices to you the rest of my life." Hearing this, the serpent couldn't help laughing. A choking smell of smoke caught it, and the serpent spat out its tongue. Realizing he had been taken in, the old man got to his feet and started to run outside. But alas, the serpent had turned the threshold into a gully. The moment the old man lifted his legs, he fell down the cliff and was killed in the gully. Instantly dark clouds gathered and lightening flashed. On the top of the hill five-coloured auspicious clouds with a celestial goddess surrounded by fairy maidens floated down and alighted slowly on the rock where Chuanhong was lying. The goddess sprayed some celestial water on Chuanhong' s face, and in a moment she came to and sat up. Seeing so many girls around her, she thought she must be in a dream. Suddenly she remembered her father and shouted towards the valley. "Daddy —" her voice rang in the valley. Just at this moment two fairy maidens with swords in their hands drove up the serpent.

The goddess raised a finger, and with a thunderbolt the serpent was chopped to death and fell eastward, turning into a foothill which is the present-day Black Dragon Hill, its bloody head the red pass. The bridge below the foothill was thus called Black Dragon Bridge.

"Daddy —" shouted Chuanhong, running and sobbing. The valley also shed tears for her. She kept running and crying. She became hoarse; she spat blood; and her tears turned into red pearls and scattered over the hills to become pears. Smoke grew out of the place where Chuanhong shed tears. When autumn came, the hills became a world of red leaves. The apricot trees dwindled, and more and more smoke trees grew.

Now on fine days in autumn, anyone gazing at the graceful red leaves on the hillsides feels as if he saw the beautiful Chuanhong again.

The Golden Pigeon Platform

ANYONE who comes to the Sleeping Buddha Temple and Cherry Gully, no matter how tired he may have been, pays a visit to the Golden Pigeon Platform.

Thirty feet high and twenty feet wide, the Golden Pigeon Platform is a hard rock with three cracks. To get to its top for the wonderful view, one has to climb the slope, but the side facing the valley is a precipitous cliff where one can stumble to one's doom.

In earlier times, on this rock once perched a pair of yellow pigeons, which glistened golden in the sunshine. Standing on the flat rock, the two pigeons now spread their wings and now held their heads high. Their each movement formed a wonderful picture. That was how people came to call them the golden pigeons and the rock the Golden Pigeon Platform. As an old saying goes, "Birds worship phoenixes", and the home of these two golden pigeons attracted larks, orioles, parrots and turtledoves. These birds sang and danced beautifully, living a happy life.

Just east of the platform lived a few poor families who had fled here to escape the heavy official taxes despite the impoverished hill soil. Strangely enough, since the golden pigeons had been here, the poor soil seemed to have been coated by a layer of oil. As long as you sowed in spring, whether on the hillsides or in the rocky cracks, you harvested in autumn. Clever villagers knew well that it was the divine help of the birds, whose droppings had actually changed the nature of the soil. Hence stories spread far and wide that the pigeons' feathers were extremely precious and that their meat could make people longlived. These stories aroused the greed of a lazy young man in the village, who made a catapult in secret.

On an extremely fine day when the birds were sporting, the young man aimed and struck the leg of a pigeon off its guard. Delighted, he threw away the catapult and scurried down the valley to catch the pigeon, but to his surprise the wounded pigeon's mate not only didn't flee but crawled beneath the wounded pigeon and lifted it with difficulty. Quickly forming a barrier in the sky, the birds nearby helped the wounded pigeon fly into the sky and disappear far over the Western Hills.

When the pigeons had left, the rock looked rather lonely. The villagers were sorry, and often took their children and grandchildren to visit it. This continued from generation to generation, and the Golden Pigeon Platform finally became one of the scenic spots of the western outskirts of Beijing.

The Twin Pool

THE Twin Pool Villa in the Fragrant Hills Park not only has beautiful scenery but also many legends. "Twin Pool" in the Emperor Qianlong's own handwriting is inscribed on the hillside west of the villa. It is said that when the capital of the Yuan Dynasty was settled in Beijing, Kublai Khan lived luxuriously and felt it a burden to administer state affairs. One day, he climbed high up in the hills and looked far out. He saw in the northwest something red as ascending fire, golden as descending clouds. "Are they celestial beings?" he wondered. He ordered his retinue to go north at once. He stopped at the Twin Pool at last. At that time, there was no villa nor any pool, only trees with red leaves which made the mountain red. Kublai Khan thought: "It was nothing but red leaves!" There were no celestials to be seen, yet Kublai Khan did not give up. He began to look for them around the hill. After three days and nights' searching, he became exhausted. When he got back to the Twin Pool he could no longer move, and leaning on a red-leafed tree, he fell asleep.

In his sleep, he dreamed of two white rabbits running to him. The rabbits jumped away from him when he tried to catch them. They jumped away again at his second attempt. They teased him by neither letting him get close to them nor running away from him. He was tempted to follow them. Though unable to catch them, he was unwilling to give up. He wondered what to do and thought of an idea. He just sat down where he was, pretending he was tired of running after them and had gone to sleep. The rabbits jumped to and fro around him and, getting nearer and nearer to him, finally climbed on to his knees. When he was sure that the rabbits were within his reach, he made a sudden attempt to catch hold of them. He felt he had them in his hands, but they slipped out again and when they got to the ground miraculously disappeared. Where the rabbits disappeared two springs gushed up, all at once billowing down upon him. This frightened him, and he shouted himself awake. He instantly ordered people to dig down beside the red-leafed tree he had leant on to sleep, and they actually found a twin pool. Kublai Khan failed to see or talk to any celestial being, but the twin pools remain and water the mountain, which is green and beautiful.

Jade Spring Mountain

JADE Spring Mountain lies approximately 2.5 kilometres west of Longevity Hill in the Summer Palace. It is a branch of the eastern spur of the Western Hills. The mountain got its name from its clear, jade-like, crystalline spring, which foams up from the bottom like boiling water. It is listed among the Eight Great Sights of Beijing. The Emperor Qianlong of the Qing Dynasty named it "The Foremost Spring Under Heaven". The Garden of Light and Tranquillity at its foot is a successful specimen of such construction with its towers, pavilions, halls, temples and pagodas built beside mountains amid springs, rocks and trees.

The Yuquan Butterflies

IN the continuously gushing spring on Jade Spring Mountain two butterflies are seen fluttering constantly in the water but not above it. From time immemorial, their shapes have been there.

Legend has it that long, long ago, the mountain had no name, nor did anyone know about the spring, until they were discovered by Jade Maiden, the daughter of the Jade Emperor, when she descended to visit the human world. Beautiful and witty, she was the Jade Emperor's favourite daughter. In the celestial palace, she had often heard stories about the human world, where there were buying and selling, and boys and girls who were happy and lively. Reaching the age of eighteen and finding the celestial palace too dull, she decided to go there.

On the eighteenth of the third lunar month she was standing at the south gate of Heaven looking down at the world, seeing beautiful women and handsome men walking in pairs under colourful umbrellas; some men followed behind women riding on donkeys; still others walked shoulder to shoulder, chatting happily. Becoming envious, she asked her maid, who told her that there was a fair at the Temple of the Goddess of the Western Hills near Beijing. The couples were going to the temple to pray to the Goddess for sons. Jade Maiden thought to herself: Wouldn't it be nice to find a husband in the world and lead a happy life?

One day, she furtively left the celestial palace and made for Jade Spring Mountain on a white cloud. She alighted at the deserted mountain top, where she sat down to rest. Tired and thirsty, she wished for a drink of water. She looked around and was overjoyed to find a spring a little way away. The clear water gushed slowly. She walked up, crouched down and drank her fill, then she sat down and tidied herself up, using the water as a mirror. She rose and looked down the mountain. It was getting dark, and cooking smoke was rising from a small village whence came the sound of chickens and dogs. She longed even more for the life of man. This mountain village seemed a good place to live, so she made directly for it. Half way down the mountain, she came across a young man coming in her direction with a load of firewood. As it was too late to hide, Jade Maiden walked straight on.

He was a pleasant-looking young man with a powerful body and regular, honest features.

The young man lived alone on the mountain amid the numerous springs, so people called him Spring Lad. He fell in love at first sight with the beautiful Jade Maiden, but mindful of his own poverty, he lowered his head and would have walked past her, had she not turned and followed behind him keeping pace.

They soon arrived at his home, where he put down his firewood and pushed open the door. Jade Maiden followed him into the hut. Silently, Spring Lad lit the stove and began to cook. Jade Maiden gave him a hand wherever she could without saying a word. When the meal was ready, he sat down to eat, as did she.

After a while, unable to restrain himself any longer, he broke the silence by asking, "Which village are you from, sister? It's getting late for you to stay with a poor young man like me."

Jade Maiden told him unhurriedly, "I'm Jade Maiden from Heaven. Now that I've left the celestial palace I can never return. Please let me stay."

Though he was overjoyed, his poverty made him protest: "You are a celestial being, while I'm a pauper. I can't let you suffer poverty with me."

"I do not mind your poverty and will never leave you if you love me truly."

Thus they lived like a devoted man and wife on the mountain, each blissful in the other's love.

Yet their happiness didn't last very long. A snake spirit on the mountain began to harbour evil designs on the beautiful Jade Maiden.

One day, fetching water from a spring, Jade Maiden flopped

down unconscious when the snake spirit blew a venomous breath over her, and she was snatched away into the snake' s den on a gust of wind.

Spring Lad was cutting firewood on the mountain. As the whirlwind rolled over him, he raised his shoulder-pole and struck out. The wind swirled three feet above the ground; a shoe dropped down and was swept along over the mountain. Spring Lad recognized the shoe as Jade Maiden's. He grabbed his axe and gave chase. Over the mountain, the wind swirled again and vanished. Spring Lad searched until he found a big, dark cave. In his eagerness to save Jade Maiden, he plunged recklessly in, fierce as a tiger. He advanced along the long, narrow passage until he came to a wider space and saw light. He noticed a stream with a sandy bank, on which was a tower. He approached and listened carefully. Nothing moved. He went a few steps nearer and saw that Jade Maiden was locked up inside. He called, "Jade Maiden! Jade Maiden!" When Jade Maiden came to, she called, "Spring Lad! Spring Lad!" He swung his axe, broke the lock and pulled her out. They fled, but the snake spirit came after them and engulfed them in a great gust of wind. Try as they might, they could not move an inch. It was as if they were stuck to the ground. Jade Maiden could not lift her feet, much as she would have liked to escape on a cloud. Turning around, they saw the snake's gory mouth gaping wide. He would soon reach them. At the last minute, Spring Lad saw a fountain beside them and plunged in with Jade Maiden.

They were changed into butterflies frolicking every day at the bottom of the water, which was called Jade Spring from then on, and the mountain was called Jade Spring Mountain. The water of the spring is forever sweet, and Jade Maiden and Spring Lad are forever in love. No one can separate them any more. They disappear when a stone is thrown into the water, reappearing as soon as it is calm.

Jade Spring's Source

ONCE upon a time there was a village called Wayao beside a pool in which floated a brown flint, rising and falling with the water like a log, called the Floating Stone. Yet it could not be got out, since it disappeared at anyone's approach.

One year, a man in his sixties came from the south. He had white hair, white eyebrows and a white beard and called himself the Three-white Old Man. He often lingered around the big pool, shaking his head and rubbing his hands at the Floating Stone. One day he fell ill on the street, foaming at the mouth and bleeding from his nose as if he was at death's door. Fisherman Zhao, named Jade Spring, returning from fishing saw the old man and carried him home, laid him on the *kang* and fed him gruel. Soon the Three-white Old Man got well. He said to Zhao, "You're a kind-hearted man, and I want to confide in you. I came from Mount Putuo in the South Sea in search of treasure. The Floating Stone in the pool is exactly what I wanted. There is a bowl of clear water inside the stone, which is dew from the celestial palace, a healing water for all diseases. It would not be difficult to get it. When an ox grazes on the roof of your hut you can just reach for it." The Three-white Old Man bid farewell to Zhao and returned to the south.

One summer it rained for a fortnight on end, and Zhao's dilapidated hut collapsed. He and his wife dug a cave at the foot of the mountain as a makeshift lodging.

When the weather cleared, Zhao took his net to go fishing in the pool. Turning around, he saw an ox come down and start to graze above his cave. Remembering what the Three-white Old Man had said, he put away his net and went to the pool to get the Floating Stone.

Zhao waded into the water and picked up the stone as lightly as if it had been a log, and it was as soft as a cooked gourd. Once home, he cut it open with a knife. In the middle was a jade bowl brimming with clear, fragrant, sweet water, which filled up as soon as it was scooped out. The joyful old couple put the Floating Stone and the jade bowl away.

An old neighbour fell ill, and she recovered instantly upon drinking some of the clear water. When the villagers learned of this, they called it magic water. Many people were cured by it. Whoever fell ill in the vicinity came to get magic water from Zhao.

The news spread far and wide until it reached the ears of the county magistrate, who asked to buy the bowl for a large sum of money. "I would not sell it for a mountain of gold or silver," said Zhao. In a rage, the magistrate ordered him to hand over the jade bowl in three days or he would send soldiers to kill Zhao and his family.

All the villagers in Wayao urged the old man to hand over the bowl and avoid this doom, but he stood his ground, saying, "He is but a petty county magistrate. I'd not obey such an order even from the Jade Emperor or the Supreme Elder Ruler. Let him cut off my head. All I'll get is a scar the size of a bowl." That night he buried the bowl at the foot of the mountain and left for Mount Putuo in the South Sea to find the Three-white Old Man.

Three days later, the magistrate and his men came in vain to get the bowl. They returned to the county town crestfallen.

When Zhao had left for the south, a spring had broken out from the foot of the mountain where he had buried the bowl. The stream, though thin, flowed continuously and was cool and sweet. To commemorate Old Man Zhao, the Wayao villagers named it the Jade Spring and the mountain Jade Spring Mountain.

Emperor Kangxi and the Rainbow over Jade Spring

WHEN Emperor Shunzhi forsook his throne and disappeared, Kangxi was made emperor at three, since "a country must have a ruler." He proved to be cleverer than most people when a boy, and eighteen years later, at 21, he knew everything about ruling a country. After Dorgun, the prince regent, died, there was only one person, Grand Secretary Aobai, who didn't think much of the Emperor. Aobai was a veteran minister who had been entrusted with the bringing up of the Emperor and one who had performed many military feats, and he often debated state affairs with the Emperor. There was also talk of his secretly gathering ministers and generals to him and probably conspiring to usurp the throne. In the eighteenth year of his reign, when Emperor Kangxi was avoiding the heat of summer at his travelling lodge on Jade Spring Mountain, Aobai, on the pretext of seeing the emperor, left the city and arrived in the Garden of Light and Tranquillity at the lodge with four subordinates.

These four men were Aobai's trusted generals, who had

fought with him for twenty years, winning many battles, and who were so well trained that they could put an arrow in the target at a hundred paces and cut the head off a commanding general amid thousands of riders. Under the pretence of seeing the Emperor, he was waiting for an opportunity to kill him and usurp his throne.

When the five men reached the foot of Jade Spring Mountain, thunder rolled in the clear sky as a black cloud approached from the northwest. A storm broke, and the sky instantly went dark. Rain fell in torrents. When it cleared a beautiful scene appeared — a fiery red sun was setting amid green mountains and streams, and a rainbow curved over Jade Spring Mountain, which seemed entirely enveloped in auspicious clouds. Aobai and his followers gaped at this wondrous sight. Taking the rainbow as the dragon image of the Emperor, they dared not approach the mountain and slunk back to the city.

The rainbow's apparition at Jade Spring Mountain became gradually known, and when the Emperor learned of it from his men, he realized that Aobai had indeed conspired against him and that he would have no peace unless he were rid of him. He had a group of young warriors trained and in three years' time asked Aobai to a banquet, where he was given a seat with only three legs. When he tipped over during the banquet, Kangxi had him killed for disrespect to the Emperor.

When Qianlong became emperor, he had a stone tablet made to record his grandfather's feats, and also, because the water in the Jade Spring did look like a rainbow in the sun, he wrote in person an inscription in four big characters reading "Rainbow Over Jade Spring". The spot was included in the Eight Great Sights of Beijing, and Jade Spring Mountain has been renowned ever since.

The Ruins of the Yuanmingyuan

THE ruins of the Yuanmingyuan are in the east of Haidian District. Originally a big imperial park in the Qing Dynasty, it was actually three separate parks: the Park of Perfection and Brightness, the Park of Everlasting Spring and the Park of Ten Thousand Springs, occupying an area of about 5,200 *mu*, with a perimeter of over ten kilometres.

The Yuanmingyuan had about a hundred and forty buildings and pavilions and about a hundred landscapes of lakes and hills, strange flowers and trees and curious stones. Most famous were the Palace of Justice and Honesty, where the emperor administered state affairs, the China Feast Palace, for the reception of guests, the Blessing Palace for sacrificial rites, the Wenyuan Pavilion for books, and the imitations of famous parks and scenes in various parts of the country such as Wuling Spring, the Three Lakes Reflecting the Moon, the Square Kettle, the Penglai Jade Palace, the Moon and Clouds and the Purple-blue House. These embodied numberless styles of gardens south of the Yangtze River and give a resume of the country's gardening in times gone by. There was also a Western-style Building. There were so many precious antiques in the park that it arms a virtual treasure-house of art and honoured as "the Park of Parks" by westerners. In 1860 it was pillaged and burned by the Anglo-French joint force. Only some engraved stones are left now.

The Western-style Building

TO celebrate his sixtieth birthday, the Emperor Qianlong ordered Guiseppe Castglione and Michel Benoist to build a Western building in the Yuanmingyuan after the style of the Chateau de Versailles. Both plunged into the work at the imperial behest. The Dashuifa, Guangshuifa and Yuanyingguan were completed immediately, but the project had to be stopped half way for lack of money. Qianlong's birthday was approaching. How disappointing it was! The Emperor called in Liu Yong to discuss the matter at once. Liu Yong, after hearing the story, thought for a moment and said, "You can easily get a hundred thousand taels of silver if you do as I tell you."

It was night when Liu Yong got home. He hurriedly sent some people out to hire eighteen camels and to buy thirty-six new bags. In Liu Yong's backyard the bags were filled with bricks and tiles, then the camels with the bags on their backs set out in the direction of the Marco Polo Bridge.

He Shen, who was an important official during Qianlong's

reign, was Liu Yong's nextdoor neighbour. He often extorted excessive taxes and levies, so he was extremely rich. On that day a servant told him that a caravan of camels with two bags of treasure each had started out from Liu's home. He Shen thought hard for a long time but could not figure out what Liu Yong was up to.

At dawn the next day, high officials hurried to the Yuanmingyuan to audience with the Emperor. After they had kowtowed to him, Qianlong said slowly:

"Today I have called you in to ask for your opinions about the Western-style Building project, because only half of the building is finished and the money has run out." The officials looked at each other, but no one could think of anything. At this moment, Liu Yong suggested to the Emperor: "Why not borrow a hundred thousand taels of silver from the officials?" He Shen suddenly understood Liu Yong's action of the night before. He thought: you have moved away all your treasure secretly, and now you are trying to have us provide the money! Oh no! He said to the Emperor, "Your Majesty, Liu Yong has committed the crime of deceiving you. He suggests that Your Majesty borrow money from the officials when he has secretly moved his treasure to his native place. That surely is deceit." Though he knew He Shen had fallen into their trap, Qianlong asked Liu Yong, "Is this true, Liu Yong?" Liu Yong answered, "I pledge my life that it is not." Turning back to He Shen, Liu asked, "What if it is not true, Official He?" He Shen replied loudly, "I will myself offer a hundred thousand taels of silver." Qianlong immediately agreed, with the other officials as witnesses. The bet was on.

Leaving the palace, He Shen sent horsemen after the eighteen camels at once. They caught up with them at noon the next day. The men and the camels were brought to the Yuanmingyuan. The thirty-six bags were opened before all the officials. To their surprise, the bags were full of bricks and tiles. There was not a single piece of gold or silver. He Shen then knew he had fallen into Liu Yong's trap and had to offer a hundred thousand taels of silver to build the Fangwangguan and the Curious Harmony Hall to complete the Western-style Building.

Taoranting Park

THE Taoranting Park, located in the southwest of Xuanwu District, is one of the biggest parks in Beijing. Back in the Liao and Jin dynasties, more than eight hundred years ago, the landscape here was like the region on the southern bank of the Yangtze River with a crisscross network of streams and lakes. In the Yuan Dynasty, an ancient temple named Benevolence Nunnery was built on a high mound. In the Ming and Qing dynasties, it became a popular spot for outings and for literati to meet together. In 1694 Jiang Zao, an official in the Ministry of Works, set up a pavilion in Benevolence Nunnery and named it Taoranting Pavilion.

The Parrot Tomb

IT is said that in early times around Benevolence Nunnery stood some bleak tombs, such as the Fragrant Tomb of a prostitute, the Drunken Guo Tomb of a famous personage, and the Parrot Tomb, which was the strangest.

How did the Parrot Tomb come to be here? We'd better begin with a small town on the shore of the South China Sea, where in the Qing Dynasty lived a poor, gifted scholar named Qiao, who was good at calligraphy and painting. His wife Yuniang was a virtuous woman. The husband and wife lived a very poor life but loved each other dearly, and their life was harmonious and happy.

Yuniang kept a parrot with snow-white feathers, so she named him Abai "Whitey". Abai was so clever and bright that he could even sing ditties, and was regarded as a pearl in the palm — a much beloved pet. In those years, any scholar aspired to high official position, and Qiao was no exception. One day he was going to Beijing to take the Imperial Examination. Yuniang worried that her husband would feel lonely on the trip and told him to take Abai with him. With sadness the two parted after exhorting each other again and again for a long time. Qiao took Abai first by boat and then by hiring beasts, and after many difficulties eventually got to Beijing. He resided in the guildhall of fellow provincials, which was located on Nanhengjie Street outside Xuanwumen Gate.

At that time the moment a rich scholar got to Beijing, he would familiarize himself with the public houses, theatres and Eight Big Lanes (where prostitutes lived), leading a life of debauchery. Qiao was self-disciplined, staying in a small room reading every day and even never going out of the guildhall. He thought himself talented and hardworking and sure to succeed. Unfortunately, due to his being unaccustomed to the climate and overtired, as soon as he entered the examination hall, his eyes grew dim, and he fainted without even touching the examination paper. He had no choice but to return to the guildhall to recuperate.

It was fortunate for him that he had the clever white parrot, who always perched beside his pillow, talking to him pleasantly. Soon Qiao regained his health.

One day Abai said to Qiao, "Master, let's go home. Madam is sure to expect your return anxiously." Qiao sighed, "In such a condition, I'd be ashamed to see her. It's better if I sit the next examination and return home when I pass." The next examination was in three years' time, and Qiao earned his living by selling his calligraphy and paintings and at the same

time studied harder. One day he heard the old gatekeeper say
that there was a temple fair, so with Abai, he took several
pieces of calligraphy and paintings and went there to sell them.
Walking out of the guildhall and south past dark kiln, he saw
Benevolence Nunnery surrounded by hillocks and reedy
ponds. It was beautiful, and Qiao was delighted. Abai flew
here and there around his master, saying teasingly, "How
beautiful it is! Why doesn't Master compose a poem?" The
words evoked Qiao's enthusiasm. He looked around him,
seeking a topic. His smile suddenly disappeared when he saw
men and women in couples and wives walking beside their
husbands, and he couldn't help heaving a long sigh.

Clever Abai read his thoughts at once and said to him,
"Master, are you missing Madam? Let me go home and see
her."

"The way is so long. Are you capable of doing that?"

"Yes," Abai replied, flapping his wings and flying up into
the sky.

From the capital to the shore of the South China Sea, Abai
had to cross nine vast mountains and twelve big rivers, and
he flew without stopping for a rest. It only took him three
days and three nights to get home.

It was fortunate that Abai came back, because Yuniang was
so anxious that she was ill. It was understandable: her husband had said that he would come back in half a year at the
most, and already half a year had passed. Of course she was
worried. The moment Yuniang saw Abai, she asked

anxiously,

"Where's your master?" Abai told her of Qiao's determination. However, Yuniang thought that Qiao probably hadn't come back because something had happened to him. She told Abai, "You go and bring your master back as soon as possible. I don't expect him to be an official as long as he loves me deafly, and we'll live our poor life together. Otherwise, I won't live any longer!"

Abai understood Yuniang, and for all that he was exhausted, he flew north again without stopping, though he was running out of energy. As he flew over a vast mountain, a ferocious vulture attacked him. Abai dodged it, and though he escaped, he left a tuft of feathers in the vulture's sharp claws; as he flew over a dense forest, a bullet hit him in the belly, and though he wasn't shot down, it largely sapped his vitality.

Abai flew back to Qiao's small room at last, and perching on the desk, he said feebly, "Madam is ill, and if Master returns earlier, maybe he can see her." Then he vomitted blood and died.

Qiao was alarmed and nervous. He chose a burial ground beside the Taoran Pavilion, buffed Abai and then left Beijing in a hurry. Over a month later, Qiao got to his home town. The couple was reunited with mixed feelings of grief and joy. Mentioning the beloved Abai, Yuniang beat her breast, crying, "If only I hadn't urged him to look for you in such a hurry!" Qiao said in deep sorrow too, "It is all my ault. I was only concerned about official position and made you worried about me and Abai exhausted to death."

From then on, Qiao didn't think about the imperial examination any longer. When his wife had regained her strength, both of them went north and visited Abai's tomb. Yuniang wept her heart out as if she had lost her own son; Qiao set up a gravestone by himself, on which were inscribed the two words "Parrot Tomb". This provided another sight in Taoranting Park, adding to its fame.

The Lama Temple

LOCATED just inside the Andingmen Gate, the Lama Temple is the biggest lamasery in Beijing. It distinguishes itself from all other temples in the city by its roofs of golden glazed tiles, the colour due only to an imperial family.

The Lama Temple was built in the 33rd year (1694) of the Kangxi Period of the Qing Dynasty as the home of the Emperor Kangxi's fourth son Yinzhen. It came to be called the Prince's Palace. When Yinzhen ascended the throne after his father died, the Lama Temple then became his imperial villa. It is said that since Emperor Yongzheng was a devout Buddhist, his successor, the Emperor Qianlong, turned the temple into a lamasery. He sent for 500 lamas from Mongolia to reside there.

The Lama Temple highlights a unique combination of the very best of Han, Mongolian, Manchu and Tibetan architecture. Its many Buddhist statues, artifacts and murals make it a treasure-house of Buddhism and its art.

The Coppersmith Han Enlivens the Copper Buddha

A six-metre-tall copper Buddha sits with a sedate smile on a lotus in the Hall of the Wheel of the Law of the Lama Temple, a sword stuck in a lotus on the statue's right shoulder and a lotus on his left shoulder holding a holy book representing wisdom and strength. This is the statue of Tsongkhapa, founder of the Yellow Sect of Buddhism.

It is said that a lama named Bai Puren of the Lama Temple collected all the 200,000 silver dollars to have the copper statue built, which when finished did not look happy. Instead it was rather solemn-looking. This worried the lamas, because Emuqi, a lama in charge of the temple's daily affairs, had opposed its making. He said to Bai, "Even the Qing Dynasty has not been able to make such a big copper statue. How can you manage it by yourself?"

So they had to try harder if they did not want to face their opponent's sneers. Supporters looked far and wide for an able coppersmith, but nobody dared to take the job. Then a lama heard that a coppersmith named Han on Temple Library

Lane near the temple had a skilful hand. Bai ordered his men to invite Han over. At that time Han was already in his seventies. After hearing the situation he said calmly, "The job is not that tough, but my legs are not up to it, and I haven't tried my hand for many years. You'd better find someone else." Desperate, one lama said hurriedly, "We can offer you a sedan-chair in that ease, and we'll pay you however much you want."

Unable to reject the offer, Han said smiling, "All right. I'll try. If I fail, you won't have to pay me a cent; if you are satisfied with my work, you'll have to pay me according to how many times I use my hammer: one stroke, one silver dollar!"

This astonished the lama, who thought to himself:

"It's too much. He may well take a couple of hundred strokes if he wants. How can we afford it?" But he had to comply with the terms in the end since he had no other choice. The next day a sedan-chair was called to carry the coppersmith to the Lama Temple, where a huge crowd had already gathered to watch. Han shouted to the crowd of lamas and onlookers, "I, Coppersmith Han, only want to leave behind some work of craftsmanship. I won't take a cent more than I deserve." Saying this, he rolled up his sleeves, took the hammer and brought it down violently yet sharply on the left cheek of the statue, then again on the right cheek. A pair of dimples appeared on the face of the statue of Tsongkhapa. The crowd could not help marvelling at the sudden change in the master's expression. "Miraculous!" "Divine!" they said.

His work finished, Han took only two silver dollars.

Today the statue of Tsongkhapa Coppersmith Han hammered is still receiving its visitors in the Lama Temple.

The Story of the *Hada*

IN lamaseries, lengths of coloured silk called hada can be seen draped on buddhas and altars. In some lamaseries even trees are draped with them. Generally speaking, there are five different colours of *hada*: white, blue, red, pink and yellow. Different nationalities use different colours. In the Hall of the Wheel of the Law in the Lama Temple a yellow hada more than a dozen metres long can be seen draped on the 15-metre-high bronze statue of the founder of the Yellow Sect of Buddhism, Tsongkhapa. This is not the longest *hada*. It is said that one over thirty metres long was once offered to the Great Buddha in the Hall of the Great Buddha. A legend tells the story of the *hada*.

Legend has it that Sakyamuni began his religious studies at twenty-nine and became a buddha after sitting quietly for six years in a deep forest. Then he went down the mountain to spread Buddhism. Many disciples, including lords and aristocrats, came long distances to listen to his teachings. In order to please the Buddha and to acquire his blessings, each one brought many gifts. They brought gold, silver and jewelry;

others brought cattle and food; some brought silk and satin. They all boasted about their gifts, believing the one with the most precious gift was the most pious. Some claimed, "The Buddha will give me satisfaction and happiness." Others claimed, "The Buddha will give me peace and good luck." Not long after, Sakyamuni arrived. One by one they presented their gifts. A poor beggar from a distant land asked the Buddha to deliver him from poverty, and misery. Seeing that everybody else had brought gifts to Sakyamuni, while he didn't even have a penny to his name or food to eat, he wondered how he could express his good wishes. He looked down at his body, which was naked except for a loincloth, and was at a loss what to do. Hesitating a minute, he scurried to the nearby river, pulled off the loincloth and washed it again and again in the water until it was very clean. Then, holding the faded rag before him in both hands, he presented it respectfully to Sakyamuni. All sneered at the naked man with the rag, but Sakyamuni was very touched and accepted it. With his hand on the man's head, Sakyamuni said, "They have given me rich presents, but this does not mean they are pious, because they have not given all they have, only a tiny part of what they have. Only you have given me all, the only thing you have. You are the most pious. No other gift is as precious as yours. I will give you peace and happiness."

This became a custom and developed into the use of different colours of *hada*, and the *hada* is regarded as the most precious gift, symbolizing luck and happiness.

Phoenix-eyed Incense Sticks

IN the Hall of the Great Buddha two huge "incense sticks" flank the great Maitreya. The sticks are 3.9 metres high with a diameter of 12 centimetres and are surrounded by a hexagonal vermilion balustrade. The incense sticks got their name because they are covered with long, narrow holes shaped like phoenixes' eyes.

Though resembling incense sticks, they are actually fossils dating back billions of years. It is said that the Tenger Desert in Inner Mongolia was once a sea of water and the fossils are those of two huge algae plants in that sea. Continuous crustal movement gradually transformed the sea into a desert. These two huge aquatic plants survived and over the years became fossils. It is also said that the two phoenix-eyed incense sticks were discovered one spring in the Qing Dynasty when a group of Mongolian merchants were crossing the Tenger Desert. On the third day, the weather suddenly changed and a violent sandstorm stopped the men and camels opening their eyes. Unable to advance any further, the merchants had to stop for a while in a pit out of the wind. The wind ravaged for three days without respite. When the merchants emerged from the pit they saw nothing but yellow sand. Even the guide could not tell which direction to take. They could only let the camels lead the way. They advanced in this way for three days and nights without getting out of the desert. On careful investigation they discovered that the camels had been going around in circles. All the rations and water they had brought were finished by then. If things went on like that the merchants could never leave the desert alive. Faced by death, many trembled and broke down; others put their hands together and prayed to the sky for the Buddha's blessing. The guide said, "We must not sit still and wait for death. I' ll go and find the way out of the desert. You wait right here." He returned when the sky was darkening and told them hopefully: "I found two huge incense sticks. They are divine incense sticks sent by Heaven. There is hope for us." Every one was exhilarated. Forgetting hunger and fatigue, they all hastened up, kowtowing again and again to the divine incense sticks. Passing between the incense sticks, the merchants advanced straight ahead until they were out of the desert and had escaped death.

The phoenix-eyed incense sticks came to be regarded as a symbol of good luck by travellers. They were looked upon as divine objects symbolizing happiness, and food and drink were presented before them.

A local lord, hearing about this, considered it a good opportunity to play up to the Qing-dynasty Emperor. He had them moved out of the desert and sent to the Emperor in Beijing. Later still they were presented by the Emperor to the Lama Temple. They are there to this day welcoming sightseers.

The Ox Street Mosque

THE mosque on Ox Street inside the Guang'an Gate is the largest and oldest mosque in Beijing. It wes built in the 13th year (AD 996) of the Shengzong Period of the Liao and was remodelled in the 7th year (1442) of the Zhengtong Period of the Ming and again in the 35th year (1696) of the Kangxi Period of the Qing. After the establishment of the People's Republic in 1949 the dilapidated mosque was remodelled again. Although it was a wooden structure in the Chinese style, its decorative motif was Arab. Inside it are a prayer hall, a minaret, a tower for observing the moon and a stele pavilion.

The Emperor Kangxi Visits
Ox Street

ORIGINALLY the mosque preserved half of an emperor's sedan-chair and an imperial edict, to which an old story is attached.

While out with his family in Ox Street, the capital Prosecutor grew suspicious seeing Moslems pouring into the mosque. It was Friday, the day of Islamic prayer. But the senile Prosecutor knew nothing about the religion. Several days later he went there again. It happened to be the Fast-breaking Festival, when during the whole month Moslems change into clean clothes and white caps after dinner and go to the mosque to pray. The Prosecutor's suspicion grew. He didn't believe such a big crowd was up to any good.

As he walked around the mosque he met a pedlar, whom he asked, "What are people doing here?"

"They follow Mohammed and gather here at night and disperse at dawn. They are very united. It is best to leave them alone," the pedlar said.

The words "They follow Mohammed" startled the

Prosecutor, who immediately wrote a report to the Emperor, claiming that the Hui people on Ox Street gathered secretly, intriguing to overthrow the Qing Dynasty. The Emperor Kangxi wondered after reading the report: the times are good, and the populace has a stable life. As no Moslem goes hungry, why do they rebel? He decided to look into the matter personally.

Usually the Emperor made a big spectacle when he travelled: an army cleared the street before him and protected him in the rear. But this time he changed into an ordinary robe and white cap. He followed the Moslems into the well-lit mosque. It was the first time he had been there. The prayer hall was grand, though less imposing than the imperial palace. In front of the hall was the minaret, an octagonal tower where the time was told. On each side of it was a stele pavilion, where ancient steles were kept. Inside the entrance was a two-storeyed building, where a tablet inscribed with "Moonwatch Tower" could be seen. Eighteen ancient cypress trees by the hall shaded a path, along which Moslems were filing into the hall, taking off their shoes to kneel respectfully on the felt. A little while later a few old robed imams in turbans appeared, one of whom began to preach on the *Koran*, Chapter 47. The Emperor Kangxi understood and made a quiet retreat.

The moment he was back, he summoned the Prosecutor, who hurried in in the hope of a promotion.

"Where did you learn the Hui people on Ox Street would rebel?" the Emperor asked.

"I saw them gathering at night. They must be planning a rebellion."

"They gather for religious rites, which have nothing to do with rebellion," the Emperor retorted.

"But a pedlar said —"

"Then where is his written complaint?"

The panicked Prosecutor stuttered, "He didn't write — but let me know verbally." The Emperor exploded with anger: "You are the capital Prosecutor but know nothing about Moslem rites. You almost trapped me with a false alarm. You are dismissed from office."

So the Prosecutor was removed from office.

Then the Emperor Kangxi issued another edict: "Hui people are perfectly justified in following their religious rites. Anyone who brings accusations out of personal revenge against the Huis' religion may be executed without my being informed."

Then the Emperor stood up and walked about in the hall, thinking: Heaven cannot have two suns or the state two rulers. Why not bestow on the Hui people half of my sedan-chair and an edict to amplify my justice and favour?

The next day half of the Emperor's sedan-chair and an inscribed edict were sent to the Ox Street Mosque with much fanfare.

The half sedan-chair was kept in the prayer hall but destroyed in 1911 when the Qing Empire fell. But the edict is still in the mosque today.

The Miaoying Temple

THE Miaoying Temple is situated in the north on Inner Fuchengmen Street and also known as the White Dagoba Temple from a white Lamaist dagoba inside. The 50.9-metre dagoba on a 9-metre base was built in the 8th year (1271) of the Zhiyuan Period of the Yuan Dynasty, While the temple was established in the 16th year. It adopted its present name in the first year (1457) of the Tianshun Period of the Ming.

The White Dagoba

THE dagoba is in Nepalese style, because of the participation of a Nepalese architect in the design. It looks like a big vase, with a 13-tiered spire. At the top of the spire stands an umbrella-like cover, on which bells are hung. The hundred and eight stone lanterns once around the dagoba are no longer there. However, the dagoba has on it seven iron hoops, about which Beijing people have a story.

The dagoba is said to be made out of one big stone. One day the dagoba began to crack, the crack on its southwest corner being about seven centimetres wide and the one on the northwest corner wide enough for a man to get in. People got anxious and whispered that the dagoba was about to collapse. Just then came a dingy old man with a sack on his back, chanting, "I fix big stuff. I fix big stuff." However, people took no notice of him. Every day anxious people gathered around the dagoba, and every day the old man came and chanted. Soon he got their attention: he didn't look like a native and had no tools with him.

"What do you fix?" a young man asked him.

"Big things."

"Woks?"

"Bigger."

"Urns?"

"Still bigger."

"Water vats?"

"Still bigger."

What can be bigger than a water vat? the young man thought. Yes, the dagoba! He pointed to the dagoba and asked, "Can you fix that?"

The old man raised his eyes, nodded, then took his leave. That night a wind rose and rain fell, and a strange sound was heard.

Early next morning people got a big surprise. The cracks in the dagoba were gone, replaced by seven iron hoops.

"The dagoba is fixed! The dagoba is fixed!" Excited people soon spread the news everywhere. People said the old man was none other than Lu Ban, and believed he had been there when the dagoba was first built.

The White Cloud Temple

THIS large and grand temple located in the Xuanwu District of Beijing was built in the 27th year (AD 739) of the Kaiyuan Period of the Tang Dynasty and was at one time the Taoist centre of north China.

The temple boasts a large collection of cultural relics, the rarest being a Tang-dynasty sculpture of Laozi and Ming editions of the *Authentic Scripture* and *Scripture of Morality*.

Tourists and Taoists have poured into the temple for rites every Spring Festival during the last several hundred years.

Magic Competition

THE White Cloud Temple was originally Buddhist and named the White Cloud Monastery. A story tells when and why the temple became Taoist and adopted its present name.

Qiu Chuji from Shandong in the Jin Dynasty learnt jade carving when he was very young and made his living from the trade after his father died. As he was kind and obliging to the poor, an immortal taught him magic and converted him to Taoism. He adopted the Taoist name Qiu Changchun and wandered about helping people. He was soon well known as an immortal.

The Yuan Dynasty succeeded the Jin. Out of reverence the Yuan Emperor invited Qiu Changchun to the capital of Beijing and granted him the title of Grand Advisor. Before long a rebellion broke out beyond Shanhaiguan Pass. Its army pushed forward, threatening the capital and throwing all the ministers into dismay. The Emperor sent Qiu Changchun to quell the rebellion, and he did it in no time with his magic. His name was on everybody's lips.

However, the Buddhist Empress became resentful. Her anger grew each time the Emperor mentioned Qiu Changchun. One day she hit upon an idea and said to the Emperor, "I have heard you mention Qiu quite often, but I have also heard of the magic power of the Buddhist Abbot Bai Yunsong of the White Cloud Temple. Why not let them compete, and we will see who is the most blessed."

"Very well, but in what way?"

"I am expecting a baby very soon," continued the Empress. "Why not send for the two and let them guess the baby's sex? We will find out very quickly."

So Qiu Changchun and Bai Yunsong were brought before the Emperor and told about the competition. Bai Yunsong, having long been resentful of Qiu Changchun, stepped forward and said first to show off:

"It will be a princess."

At this the Emperor turned to Qiu Changchun, "Now your turn."

Qiu Changchun smiled, "It will be a prince."

"Though I am limited in magic," Bai Yunsong argued, "how can I be wrong on such an easy matter as this? If I am wrong I will give my monastery to Qiu Changchun."

Still smiling, Qiu Changchun answered, "I have no temple to give away if I am wrong, but my head will be my gage."

The day the Empress gave birth, both Qiu Changchun and Bai Yunsong were summoned to a side hall, where they waited together with the Emperor. In the evening a eunuch came, reporting that the Empress had given birth to a princess. Bai Yunsong smiled a contented smile.

The Emperor turned to Qiu Changchun in embarrassment, but Qiu Changchun still smiled, saying, "I would like to see with my own eyes. Then I am willing to die if I am wrong."

The Emperor immediately sent for the baby, who was brought in by a eunuch. Qiu Changchun walked up and gently opening the swaddling clothes said, "Please have a look, Your Majesty." Then a cry was heard from the eunuch: "Yes, Qiu the Immortal is right. It is indeed a prince."

Qiu Changchun had not of course failed to tell the baby's sex, but in order to get the upper hand he purposely announced it was male and with his magic power turned the baby into a male the moment he opened the clothes. Though seeing through Qiu's trick, Bai Yunsong was unable to foil it. He could do nothing but admit defeat and give his temple to Qiu Changchun. After remodelling the temple, Qiu Changchun moved in and changed its name to the White Cloud Temple.

Bai Yunsong would not give up after the loss of face before the Emperor. He built a monastery to the west of the White Cloud Temple and named it the Western Wind Monastery, in the hope of "blowing the white cloud before the western wind". Every evening he stood in his monastery holding a peach-wood sword. At his incantations and a swish of his sword, instant wind rose. It carried sand and stones against the White Cloud Temple. However, Qiu Changchun wouldn't take this seriously: he just built in his temple a Wind-subduing Cave and a Wind-sheltering Bridge. They both drained the force of the wind before it could do any harm. Seeing his trick fail, Bai Yunsong became yet angrier. However, Qiu Changchun made peace by visiting the Western Wind Monastery, saying to Bai Yunsong, "There is no inveterate conflict between Taoism and Buddhism. If you are willing to help people, I will give your monastery back." Seeing he could never get the upper hand and also touched by Qiu Changchun's good faith, Bai Yunsong dispelled his resentment and left to wander about the world.

Since then the White Cloud Temple has been well known to everybody, while the Western Wind Monastery has dilapidated into nothing.

The Great Bell Temple

IN Haidian in the northwestern suburbs of Beijing there is a big temple formerly known as the Temple of Awakening. Since the famous great bell it houses was moved there it has been called the Great Bell Temple. Cast in 1406 in the Yongle Reign of the Ming, the bell is 6.94 metres high, 22 centimetres thick and weighs 46.5 tonnes. The lip is 3.3 metres in diameter. On the bell are inscribed 17 Buddhist sutras totalling 227,000 characters, which are believed to be in the hand of Shen Du, a calligrapher of the Ming. The exquisitely cast bell is famous not only for its size but also for its pure, deep and melodious tone. Its clear sound can be heard twenty kilometres away. The Great Bell Temple has become a museum of bells of past dynasties.

The Great Bell

LONG long ago, there lived an old man who specialized in casting bells. He went wherever a bell was to be cast. He had a beautiful, clever daughter who followed him wherever he went. When she was eighteen, the girl was engaged to a young man from a founder's family in Tongzhou near Beijing, and they were going to get married the next year.

That year the Emperor wanted to build a huge bell tower in Beijing. The old man was recruited to be the head of the builders, and his daughter's wedding was held up.

At that time a drum tower had already been built in Beijing to tell the time, but there had to be a bell tower to match it, so the Emperor ordered the bell tower built and a huge bell weighing over 10,000 *jin* cast. Founders from all over the country were summoned, including the young man from Tongzhou. To cast it, a foundry was set up to the west of the Drum Tower, where several hundred people worked hard day and night.

However, no matter how hard they worked, they could not cast the big bell. This desperately worried the old man, who moaned and groaned every day. Noticing this, his daughter was deeply worried too.

Soon time was up. The old man went to the factory very early that day. Unable to remain idle at home, his daughter followed him hastily to the factory. When she got there, she saw the fire licking the sky and all the craftsmen drenched in sweat, bustling about, while her father was organizing the last casting. Crucibles of molten bronze were being poured into the hill-like mould, but the metal did not solidify. All the builders were desperately worried, not knowing what to do.

Just then the girl suddenly remembered the saying that "Molten bronze can only solidify when it meets human blood." So she decided to sacrifice herself in order to save her father and his mates, because the Emperor would have them killed if they failed to cast the bell. She ran up to them and cried loudly: "Here I am, dad!" And with that she jumped into the furnace. The molten bronze splashed in all directions amidst blue light. All the craftsmen were dumbfounded.

The old man ran up to save her, but it was too late. He only found an embroidered shoe beside the furnace.

The great bell was thus cast. Its sound was particularly clear and melodious and could be heard clearly from many miles away. When it was tolled, it was given eighteen quick strokes, eighteen slow strokes and eighteen quick-and-slow strokes, and people called the girl the Bell-casting Lady. This is the huge bell housed in the Temple of Awakening, known as the King of Chinese Bells.

How the Great Bell Was Moved

WAS the big bell in the Great Bell Temple cast there on the spot? No. It was moved there from another place. Here is the story:

When the Prince of Yan, Zhu Di, became emperor, he was afraid of being overthrown. In order to eliminate all rebellion, he sent his counsellor Yao Guangxiao to gather all knives, spears and other weapons from the common people to have them cast into a huge bell 87,000 *jin* in weight. It was inscribed with the Avatamsaka Sutra. It was said that no one would rise in rebellion after hearing the sound of the bell, but later, for some reason, the bell sank into the canal in front of Wanshou Temple outside the Xizhimen Gate and remained there for over a hundred years during the late Ming and early Qing. No one thought to raise it, so the big bell gradually faded from memory.

One day, an old fisherman discovered a big bell sunk in the canal, and the news spread quickly to the ear of the Qing Emperor, who ordered his Minister of Works to raise it and move it to the Temple of Awakening to be hung in a tower. Acting upon the Emperor's order, the Minister sent people to raise the bell. It was not too difficult to get it up from the bottom of the canal, but nobody knew how to move so heavy a bell to the temple five or six miles away. The bell was raised in the summer, but by late autumn no one had found a way to move it. The Minister came to reprimand them, but the diggers still could not do a thing, although they racked their brains. They were all very annoyed.

It began to drizzle in September, and the bell diggers got more annoyed, so they pooled their money together to get drinks in their workshed, using a slabstone as their table. The foreman sat at one end of the stone, while the others crowded around him, regardless of the water dripping from the ceiling. The foreman lifted his cup and asked his men to drink with him, but the more he drank, the more vexed he got, so he passed his cup to the man sitting at the other end of the stone to drink it up for him. In his haste he dropped his cup on to the floor and spilt the wine. Everyone regretted this. Just then a man nicknamed Mute said, "The cup was too slippery. You should have pushed it to him over the surface of the stone!" Taking no notice of him, the workmen went on drinking in silence, until one man jumped up all of a sudden, clapping his hands. "That's it!" he cried. "The Mute is right!" Then he explained: "Suppose the cup is the big bell. If we dig a small canal from here to the temple and fill it with water, when the water freezes in winter, we can push the bell over the ice.

Isn't our problem solved?" Everyone agreed it was a good idea, and after further discussion they reported it to their superiors the next day. Soon their plan was adopted, the land was levelled, and a small canal was dug. When the water froze, the big bell was moved over the ice to the temple.

The Sleeping Buddha Temple

FORMALLY named the Temple of Circuitous Enlightenment, this is located to the south of Longevity and Peace. Hill, which stretches north of the Fragrant Hills and the Azure Clouds Temple. It was constructed during the Zhenguan Reign of the Tang Dynasty and gained its present name in 1734, when it was renovated. The main buildings, which follow each other southwards, are the Devaraja Hall of Buddhas of the Three Ages, the Sleeping Buddha Hall and the two-storeyed hall for Buddhist scriptures. In the Sleeping Buddha Hall lies the Buddha, cast in 1321 from 250,000 kilos of bronze. Behind him stand twelve statues of his disciples, as when Sakyamuni delivered his death-bed admonitions. On the left before the hall rise two saltrees said to have been brought from India at the foundation of the temple.

Sakyamuni and the Sleeping Buddha Temple

THE Sleeping Buddha Hall is at the very back of the temple. The statue of Sakyamuni lies sleeping peacefully on one side with his left hand along his leg and his right hand holding his chin. Behind it is a row of the twelve disciples modelled in clay.

The tale goes that one day, when Sakyamuni passed the Fragrant Hills on a trip around the country, he was fascinated by the beautiful green hills and clean waters and decided to have a little stroll around, but he found the crops in the fields were dying and the farmers all looked depressed. He managed to ask some passersby and learned that twelve demons wanted to own this place and were pressing the residents to move immediately. The residents, however, having lived there for generations, refused to go.

The demons found it hard to persuade the farmers and resorted to witchcraft. They produced nauseating air, which killed the crops and made the farmers ill.

The Great Buddha was furious at this. He quickly set out

to visit the demons and told them to leave right away. They ignored the plain-looking monk, which led to a trial of strength. They agreed that if Sakyamuni lost, he would be the lifelong slave of the demons, whilst if the demons were defeated, they should join the Buddha's retinue for ever and stay up to recite sutras even when Sakyamuni was asleep.

The demons were no match for Sakyamuni and quickly at their wits' end. Sakyamuni pointed one finger at the sky and down poured a shower of rain, washing away the demonic air. The crops turned green, and the farmers felt well again.

Sakyamuni felt tired, lay down on a huge stone and went to sleep. The twelve demons, though exhausted too, had to stand humbly by the sleeping Buddha, murmuring the sutras. This was their punishment from Sakyamuni for their bad treatment of the farmers.

Since then, the Fragrant Hills have been much greener, and the stream water is much cleaner. Each year there is a good harvest. To express their gratitude to Sakyamuni the farmers built a temple — today's Sleeping Buddha Temple — in the hope that Sakyamuni would stay for ever and protect the people nearby. They also cast twelve statues of the demons in order to have them meditate day and night.

Tanzhe Monastery

FORTY kilometres west of Beijing, Tanzhe Monastery stands on Tanzhe Hill with its steps leading upward to a magnificent view of the halls. Nine mountain peaks in the background, gurgling streams in front, ancient pagodas, pine trees and slender bamboos make the place a wonderful summer resort for tourists.

As the saying goes: "Tanzhe Monastery was built before Beijing. The monastery, originally named Jiafu, was first built in the Jin Dynasty, while Beijing dates from its days as the capital of Yuan Dynasty, some 800 years later.

In the monastery there is a 30-metre-high tree with a four-metre diameter. It takes ten people to circle the Liao-dynasty ginkgo tree, named the Emperor by the Emperor Qianlong of the Qing Dynasty, as its younger neighbour of the same species was named the Minister.

Legend has it that every time the Qing Dynasty had a new emperor a new trunk began to grow from the root of the first tree, from which it got its imperial name.

The "Praying Brick" is believed to have belonged to Princess Miaoyan of the Yuan, a daughter of Kublai Khan, when she was a nun there. It is said that the marks on the brick are her footprints.

The Magic Pot

OLD people in Beijing know that there is a big copper pot, an heirloom, in Tanzhe Monastery. Legend says that porridge cooked in this pot can feed any number of people.

At one time monks were only acknowledged as such after being initiated in a big temple like Tanzhe Monastery. At every initiation monks poured into it hoping to be accepted. They never came empty-handed. Every one would bring some grain along. Grain came by cart and on backs and piled up in the monastery.

One year a severe drought caused a famine, and people from far and wide came and surrounded Tanzhe Monastery in desperation, knowing of its grain store and hoping for charity. On the day of the initiation, more than 500 starving peasants gathered outside. With the monks and postulants inside the monastery, there were more than 1,000 people to be fed. Everybody looked to the abbot for food and water, particularly the peasants. Porridge was the only solution to stave off hunger and quench thirst. Although the big copper pot could contain two basketfuls of rice, it was still too small for the crowd. The monks had to bring out the monastery's biggest pot, two metres deep and with a diameter of more than three metres. It could cook at least twenty baskets of rice at one time. Even that big a pot would have only half fed the monks and the peasants.

Tanzhe Monastery's charity porridge drew more local peasants, and its rice was eaten up quickly. The old abbot was at his wits' end. How could the remaining rice last for the 53 days of the initiation? And they certainly could not ignore the starving peasants. Salvation and charity were Buddhist virtues. But where could they get grain? In the end the monks had to eat less to leave more food for the peasants.

What they feared most happened at last: on the 50th day of the initiation they ran out of food. If they wound up the initiation hastily, the monastery's good name would be ruined, not to mention the number of peasants there were to save.

The old abbot was almost in tears when he saw the last pot of porridge. He stamped his foot and ascended to the Heavenly Hall. He knelt down in front of the Buddha and kowtowed loudly, praying for grace.

There were two green snakes, the long Big Green and the short Small Green, in the Heavenly Hall. It was said that they were the servants of the Buddha. They ofen lay on the altar, and the monks of Tanzhe Monastery revered them. As the old abbot was asking for help, he saw Big Green stretch its neck out and nod to him. He was confused. A moment later Big

Green crawled down to the ground and slid out of the hall. The abbot was too worried to notice its disappearance. Soon a novice monk ascended to the Heavenly Hall and stuttered, "Master, a miracle! A miracle!"

"What has happened?" the abbot turned and asked him. The monk said, "We usually finish the porridge when the people have eaten, but today when everybody's finished the pot still brims with gruel. Isn't that magic?" Hearing this, the abbot walked quickly out of the hall and dashed to the kitchen.

When he got there the kitchen was packed with people discussing the miracle curiously. He elbowed his way forward and found the pot brimful of porridge. He asked those around him, "Have you all eaten?" "Yes, quite enough," they answered. He walked over to the pot and ladled a bit of gruel into his mouth. Ah, it tasted good!

It was only three days later, when the initiation was finished, that the gruel was all eaten. At the bottom of the pot they found a little pile of bones. Some said they were a bird's, and others said they looked like a chicken's. When the abbot came up and looked, he cried, "Ah, Heaven!" and walked quickly away. It reminded him of Big Green. He rushed to the altar in the Heavenly Hall and found only Small Green there. He searched everywhere for Big Green, but not a trace of it was found. Small Green stretched out its neck on the altar and wept: Big Green had cooked himself in the pot.

Ever since then the pot has been a Tanzhe Monastery heirloom.

The Dragon Spring Temple

THE Dragon Spring Temple stands at the feet of the mountains 1.5 kilometres west of Xibutou, northwest of Xishan Farm in Haidian District, facing south. It is not known when it was founded, but the trees at the gate date back to the Liao and Jin dynasties, and the bridge at the source of the Yuhe River nearby was built in the mid-seventeenth century. The cypress tree in the temple is 300 years old, so the foundation is tentatively put at the end of the Ming or beginning of the Qing Dynasty. Originally there were two groups of buildings: that facing east is ruined, and that facing south has some forty dilapidated rooms, as yet unrestored, while the murals in the main hall still await cataloguing. The temple stands on a cliff with a dragon head at each end of the ridge. It is now owned by Xishan Farm.

The Legend of Lord Wei

OLDWei was a hired hand for the landlord in Qiansha Ravine. He was tall and strong, his palm was as big as a dustpan, and his foot might have been more than 20 inches long. He ate pounds of dough per meal and even ten young men together could not match him at field work. One summer, when the sun was very hot, the landlord still told Old Wei to hoe the sorghum fields. Outraged, Old Wei laid all but five shoots, one in the middle and the other four around it. The landlord was desperate when he saw the other seedlings on the ground as dry as hay. He bellowed: "I feed you and pay you to do me a good job. Now you ruin me!" Old Wei replied flatly: "Oh, you blame me for leaving too many shoots!" He picked up the hoe and destroyed four more. The landowner was almost at his wits' end. Old Wei smiled: "Master, this one alone promises a harvest."

When harvest time came, the sorghum had grown to the height of a two-storeyed house, and its grain was as red as an autumn maple. Old Wei leant a ladder against its trunk and told the landlord: "You just need two knocks on the trunk, and it'll drop five thousand kilos. Remember: don't be greedy." The landlord could not wait but hurried up the ladder and gave more than twenty knocks on the trunk. A mountain of grain piled up on the ground burying both the sorghum tree and the greedy landlord.

From then on, Old Wei was no longer a hired hand. He moved to the mountains and passed his days there. He was generally considered an immortal, and a gilded statue of him was built. He was honoured as Lord Wei, and his burial site was named Lord Hill. He died on August 17, the day on which he rose to heaven. In following years, people nearby gathered to pay anniversary homage to him and place a pair of shoes exactly his size under the altar. Next year would find the soles thinner. Surely Lord Wei had worn them out with hard work.

Black Dragon Pool

BLACK Dragon Pool, located in a four-kilometre-long valley with a drop of 220 metres north of Lupiguan in Shicheng Township, Miyun County and 100 kilometres from Beijing, has three falls and eighteen ponds. The water of the falls seems to drop out of the sky, tumbling over precipitous, knife-edge cliffs and spattering into a haze, while the ponds themselves are deep green, and from their brinks peaks tower into the sky, framing the falls in a breath-taking spectacle. Grotesquely-shaped, jagged rocks, secluded paths and gurgling springs confront the eye in infinite variety, and when the autumn wind sends the foliage flying, the wild geese rest here on their way south. The True Black Dragon Pool is round and five metres across, dark green and fathomless, serene and desolate, magnificent and mysterious. One must visit it to know the bite of its cool.

In recent years Black Dragon Pool has become one of the most popular scenic spots in Beijing.

The Fight Between the Black and White Dragons

LEGEND has it that when Gao Liang drove the Dragon Father, the Dragon Mother, the Dragon Son and the Dragon Daughter to the foot of Mount Yuquan, he speared the Dragon Daughter. The Dragon Mother seized the wounded Dragon Daughter and fled to Black Dragon Pool north of the mountain. Soon the Dragon Daughter's wound healed.

One day when the Dragon Daughter was picking wild-flowers, a young man, dressed all in white with a circular dragon-shaped hat, came up to her. "Little girl, do you know me?" he asked. "Yes, you're the White Dragon," answered the Dragon Daughter. Laughing heartily, the White Dragon continued, "It's good that you know me, but do you know to whom that pool belongs?" "How can you say a pool's one person's and not another's?" "It was granted to me by the Emperor, so it's mine. You can't live here," said the White Dragon. Curling her lip, the Dragon Daughter retorted, "It belongs to those who live here. We will stay!" "Only if you go and ask for your mother's consent to marry me and be my wife," said the White Dragon, grinning hideously. The Dragon Daughter swung her emerald-green jade earrings and turned to run towards the pool. "Stop, little girl. You tell your mother I live in White Dragon Pool, north of yours. I give you three days for an answer. If you fail, I'll fight her!" shouted the White Dragon after her. Back in the pool, the Dragon Daughter told all that had happened, and the Dragon Mother was angered.

Aware that the mother and the daughter wouldn't agree, the White Dragon once again changed into a young man in a white hat and clothes and went to the village. "I am the Dragon King," he said to the villagers. "In three days' time, I'll spar with a wild dragon from Black Dragon Pool, and you'll see two columns of water in the sky, one black and one white. The white one will be me. When you see the white column fall, you must quickly throw buns into White Dragon Pool. If I win, I'll bring you good weather; if I lose, don't blame me for drowning the whole village." The villagers complied.

The Dragon Mother called all the fish together and said to them, "I intend to settle down here and be your neighbour, but now the evil dragon in White Dragon Pool wants to fight me. I need provisions, but what am I to do? I have no alternative but to make use of you. If I win, I'll return your lives; if I lose, my daughter will do so." The fish dared not utter a word, and the Dragon Mother swayed and turned into a long black dragon, which opened its mouth and sucked all the fish into its stomach.

When the third day came, a thunderbolt cracked the clear sky. A shining white column of water rose from White Dragon Pool and headed straight towards Black Dragon Pool, from which leapt a jet-black column. The columns entwined in the sky for three days and nights. The white one fell from time to time for lack of strength and soon rose when it had eaten enough buns, but the black column never dropped. The fight didn't stop until the third evening, when the columns withdrew simultaneously into their pools with a loud crack, leaving two dead dragons at the foot of the mountain. Both the White Dragon and the Dragon Mother had run out of strength and died. The Dragon Daughter grieved to see her mother dead, but she had to return the lives of the fish. She set her feet, dashed herself against a rock in the pool and was instantly shattered to pieces, which fell into the pool and turned into a kind of fish with a wide tail and long fins. This kind of fish blazed with colour in the sunshine. People say this was taken to come from the Dragon Daughter's embroidered dresses; the two emerald-green dots on the gills were her earrings. The fish usually hid beneath the rocks in the pool, which was interpreted in the light of the Dragon Mother's warning to her daughter not to venture out of the water. Since they could bump their heads against the rocks, if you put one in a fish bowl with pebbles in, it would make a rustling sound. People say this was because the Dragon Daughter was thinking of her mother. This kind of fish is called the "cloth fish".

No dragon has lived here since the Dragon Father, the

Dragon Mother and the Dragon Daughter died, but White Dragon Pool and Black Dragon Pool survive as names.

The Ten Crossings

THE Ten Crossings, situated on the middle and upper reaches of the Juma River, are a famous scenic spot of Beijing.

Leaving Zhangfang, the river meanders across the sixth, seventh, eighth and ninth crossings and finally reaches the so-called tenth crossing, where it flows smoothly and steadily in a wide valley, and the steep cliffs and grotesque rocks on the banks flicker in the morning fog, dark in the distance and bright nearer to, like a splashed-ink painting. Between the bank and the green mountains sit small villages with rough stone walls and gravel lanes. At sunset, wisps of smoke rise from the village chimneys, and the green mountain ranges are reflected in the river. This combination of poetry and painting enjoys the reputation of being the Northern Guilin Landscape.

Scarlet Girl Ferry

A stream meanders through Maan, Scarlet Ferry and finally falls into the Juma River. Scarlet Ferry was originally named Scarlet Girl Ferry, which was changed to Scarlet Port for convenience. Why was it named Scarlet Girl Ferry?

In legend there once was a young man named Chunshan, who worked for the landlord Skew-eye Wang in the fields with his father. The father and son toiled and sweated day and night no matter whether it was scorching summer or cold winter. One year, after the grain had been threshed and put in the storehouses, the father and son were about to take their yearly rest when the evil-hearted Skew-eye Wang hid his straw cutter secretly and insisted that Chunshan's father had stolen it.

Chunshan's father struck his chest: "Poor I may be, but I do have a backbone. You can't slander me like this!"

Skew-eye Wang bribed the police and had Chunshan's father arrested. He died in prison. Chunshan fumed with rage, but he could do nothing about it. He struck a match and set the landlord's house on fire and fled deep into the mountains.

Chunshan hauled rocks and stones, built a house and settled down. Having failed to find any wild fruit for several days on end, he was suffering from severe hunger and cold when a coloured cloud suddenly floated down. He had long heard the old people say that there was treasure where coloured clouds descended. He climbed to the top of the mountains, where his eyes were hurt by a red light. Rubbing his eyes and watching carefully, he found it was a little bird with bright red feathers, curled up on the snow, frozen. He picked the bird up and gently wiped away the snowflakes from its body. Unbuttoning his ragged cotton-padded jacket, he placed it against his chest.

The minute Chunshan got home, he put the little bird on the warm *kang* and covered it with quilting.

"You go to sleep. I'll make some hot soup for you!" he said soothingly.

The flame crept into the flue of the *kang* and shone upon Chunshan's face. He cooked a bowl of birch-leaf pear soup and mouthed it into the little bird's beak. The bird opened its eyes and nodded continuously just like a human being.

With the bird there, Chunshan forgot his hunger and cold and became spirited. The second day, he not only picked some wild fruit, but also dug a ginseng plant from a crack in the cliff. Worrying about the bird, he started home happily. After crossing a mountain, he looked in the direction of the stone house. Alas, how come smoke was rising from it?

When he got back he noticed that the wooden door was still latched with a stick. He entered the house and went to see the little bird and found it lying on the *kang* with its eyes closed. He lifted the pot lid and saw steaming hot noodle soup, which smelt delicious.

From then on, each time Chunshan came back from the mountains, food had been prepared, and the wild fruit and herbs he collected had also miraculously increased.

Soon it was the twelfth month of the lunar year. Chunshan put the herbs into a basket and went to the fair down the mountains. Having sold the herbs, he looked up and saw Skew-eye Wang coming surrounded by his henchmen. He turned, fought his way out of the crowd and hurried home.

He saw the smoke over the stone house far in the distance. Going behind the house and watching through a crack in the stone wall, he discovered a beautiful girl in a cotton-padded jacket and long skirt making dumplings. He murmured to himself: "Where did she come from?" And tiptoeing round to the front, he pushed open the door, rushed in, bowed deeply and asked, "May I know who you are?"

The girl blushed and returned the bow, saying, "I am the little bird you saved."

"Ah!" Half in disbelief, Chunshan clambered on to the *kang* to find the little bird, only to find a shining feather robe. He took it in his hands and asked bewildered, "What is this?"

"Please give it back to me!"

"Why?"

"I was a celestial maid in heaven. For breaking the rules of Heaven, I was turned into a bird and exiled to the earth. To thank you for saving my life, I secretly boiled water and cooked meals for you. If you don't return my robe, I won't be able to fly back to the sky !"

They got married and led a happy life.

The day after Skew-eye Wang saw Chunshan in the market, he sent people into the mountains for information. Learning that the poor fellow had married a beauty, he became extremely envious. With torches and weapons, he led his henchmen into the mountains.

Chunshan, still collecting herbs in the mountains, felt the bird robe inside his cotton-padded jacket jumping. Worrying about his wife, he started to run home. When he got there there was no sign of her, the wooden door was broken, and the pots smashed. He started to run like a madman, shouting: "Scarlet Girl! Scarlet Girl!"

Skew-eye Wang tied the girl's hands and feet with hemp rope, then ordered his henchmen to carry her on stout carrying poles. Just as they started down the mountains they heard Chunshan's shouts.

"Chunshan! Chunshan!" the girl shouted back at the top of her voice.

Skew-eye Wang skewed his eyes, and an evil idea occurred to him. He ordered the henchmen to stop and wait for Chunshan, catch him and bind him.

Following the girl's shouts, Chunshan came closer and

closer. Skew-eye Wang waved his staff, and the henchmen surged forward. Just as they were about to catch him, they heard Scarlet Girl shout wildly,

"Stop!"

The thunderous shout stunned the henchmen to their very souls. They looked up and around and saw that Chunshan and Scarlet Girl had turned into beautiful rocks on top of the mountain. One had a bunch of herbs in his left hand and was waving his fight hand and shouting. The other had long, flowing hair and a skirt and was running toward Chunshan with open arms. When they turned to look for Skew-eye Wang, he had turned into a stone in the river, and it looked as if it was sticking up its bottom to be stamped on by passers-by.

In memory of Chunshan and Scarlet Girl, later generations called this place Scarlet Girl Ferry. According to some people, when clouds and fog cap the valley, the shouts of the young couple can still be heard.

Phoenix Ridge

LOCATED in the east of the Western Hills, this is close to the Western Hills Farm and accessible by bus from Haidian along the Anhe River. It towers up into the clouds and is dark, as few trees remain. On the top of the hill is a flat square of stone in the shape of a tall building with a balcony. On it sits a rock, shading the whole platform.

Shade Rock

ONCE upon a time, there was a young man who often went to Phoenix Ridge to cut firewood. One day, when he climbed up to the balcony-like stone, he found two hale and hearty old men playing chess attentively. The young woodcutter, being a chess lover himself, put down his shoulder pole and axe and started to look on. Soon he got lost in the game and forgot all that he had come for. As the sun rose higher, it turned hotter. One of the old men picked up a little stone and placed it on the southern part of the balcony. Surprisingly, the stone grew to a huge, house-size stone, shading them from strong sunlight. And much stranger was that no matter from which direction the sun shone it could not reach the players.

At noon, the other old man drew out a pear, and they shared it as lunch. Then they dropped the core on the ground. The young man was very hungry now, so he picked up the core and swallowed it. A while later the game was finished, and the two old men left. The woodman recalled his firewood and turned back for his tools, which were already rotten.

Slowly he went back to his village, where he was astonished to see everything entirely different from how it had been. He himself, at the same time, had become a sheer stranger. Then he realized he had met two immortals on the stone.

Lugou Bridge

LUGOU Bridge, of stone, spanning the Yongding River 15 kilometres southwest of Beijing, is one of the longest ancient arched bridges surviving in north China. It was first built in 1189 but destroyed by flood in the Kangxi Period of the Qing. Rebuilt in 1698, the present structure is 266.5 metres long, 7.5 metres wide and supported by 11 arches. Along each side is a balustrade, and on each of its 140 balusters is a white marble lion. There are 485 of these lifelike lions on the whole of the bridge, and as a Beijing saying has it, "The lions on Lugou Bridge are uncountable." At the eastern end of the bridge stands a pavilion in which is a white marble stele with the inscription "The Morning Moon over Lugou" taken from the handwriting of the Emperor Qianlong of the Qing. Greatly admired by the Italian traveller Marco Polo 700 years ago, the bridge has a further claim to fame as the site of the "July 7 Lugou Bridge Incident". It was here that on July 7, 1937 the Japanese imperialists fired the first shot of their full-scale invasion of China.

The Uncountable Lions

THERE are two balustrades on the bridge, and on each baluster is a white marble lion, the big ones having smaller ones on them. They are extremely lifelike, either rampant or couchant. Some thrust forth their chests to gaze at the sky; some stare fixedly at the bridge; some turn to face their neighbours as if to chat; some fondle their cubs as if calling softly to them. Each has its own features, and how many there are no one can tell.

Legend has it that once a newly-appointed magistrate in Wanping County where the bridge is located would not believe it when he was told that the lions on Lugou Bridge were uncountable. That can't possibly be true, he said to himself.

One day he summoned all the garrison troops stationed in the county town and said to them, "They say the lions on the bridge are uncountable. Today I'm sending all of you to count them. If you can do so, you'll be rewarded, but mind you all get the same number."

The soldiers went to the bridge, formed a line and began to

count along the balustrades. They counted with each step they took, each silently to himself. When they had done they compared the results, and each was different. When this was reported to the magistrate, he said, "You must do it again." So the soldiers went back and did as they were ordered.

This time they did it more carefully, three times in succession, but when they met at the end of the bridge and compared figures, the result was no better. The magistrate was very angry and gave each of the soldiers a sound telling off.

"If you are not convinced, sir, go and count them yourself," they retorted.

Easy, thought the magistrate to himself: I will, and see how I'll treat you when I know the right number!

He took a sedan-chair to the bridge, got out and started counting from the eastern end to the western end and then back again, once, twice — but no matter how many times he counted, he never got the same number once. Finally he was so tired that sweat poured from his forehead and his back and legs were aching. He had to give up and retreat.

In bed that night he could not get to sleep: Why are the lions uncountable? Is it because they can move about on their legs? At this thought he rolled out of bed and went back to the bridge.

It was midnight, and the world was at peace except for the gurgling of the river beneath the bridge. The magistrate tip-toed on to the bridge and found to his surprise that all the lions were gambolling about, dashing helter-skelter and jumping on and off the railings, the smaller ones rolling back and forth on the backs of the bigger ones. The lively scene made him catch his breath, at the sound of which all the lions, big and small, rushed back to their positions on the balusters and crouched there still and silent.

They had in fact been carved by Lu Ban when the bridge was built, and when he had finished them he had given each a blow on the head with his hammer so that they would run about on the bridge at night but never leave it.

This is why, they say in Beijing, the lions on Lugou Bridge are uncountable.

Old Beijing

BEIJING is located in the northern apex of the North China Plain, surrounded by the Bohai Sea 150 kilometres to the east, the Taihang Mountains to the west, Juyongguan Pass to the north and Heji to the south, a city richly endowed by nature.

In the early Western Zhou Dynasty (1066- 771 BC) small settlements appeared southwest of the present site of Beijing. After the overthrow of the Shang Dynasty, King Wu of Zhou adopted the feudal system, and eventually seventy-one feoffs were granted, of which Yan, under the Duke of Shao, became more and more powerful and prosperous. He expanded his territory to Jicheng (predecessor of Beijing) and made this the capital of Yan, hence the name Yanjing still used sometimes today. When Qín Shi Huang unified China, Jicheng became the capital of Guangyang Prefecture, a northern city with strategic importance. In the Sui Dynasty it was the capital of Zhuojun Prefecture, and in the Tang Dynasty it belonged to Youzhou Prefecture, so it was also called

Youzhoucheng (the City of Youzhou). In the Liao Dynasty it was designated a secondary capital, named Nanjing. In 1153 the city was made the capital of the Jin Dynasty and renamed Zhongdu (Central Capital). Kublai Khan, founder of the Yuan Dynasty, built a new capital on the site and named it Dadu (Great Capital). From then on the city served as the political centre of all China. In 1368 Zhu Yuanzhang established the Ming Dynasty in Nanjing then went north and captured Dadu, calling it Beiping. It was renamed Beijing by Emperor Chengzu of the Ming, who moved the capital there in 1420. In 1644 Emperor Shunzhi made it the capital of the Qing Dynasty, keeping it as the centre of politics, culture and economics. As a capital Beijing goes back more than 800 years.

Beijing, a city world-famous for its long history, ancient culture, wonderful scenery, many antiquities and glorious revolutionary tradition, attracts many Chinese and foreign visitors.

The Eight-Armed Nezha City

EVERYONE calls Beijing the Eight-armed Nezha City.* They say only eight-armed Nezha could have subdued the vicious dragons in Bitter Sea Waste. Well, how did Beijing come to be built as an Eight-armed Nezha City? There's a folk-tale about this.

The Emperor decided to build a northern capital, Beijing,** and entrusted this task to the Minister of Works. That threw the minister into a panic. He promptly petitioned the throne: "Beijing was originally known as the Bitter Sea Waste, and the dragons there are too vicious for your humble subject to overcome. I beg Your Majesty to send some military advisers

---

* Nezha, a mythical boy with supernatural powers, killed the son of the Dragon King. Later he disembowelled himself and cut the flesh from his bones; but his spirit took the form of a lotus, and he continued to battle with and overcome many evil spirits.

** The inner city of Beiing was built in 1267 in the Yuan Dynasty. In 1368, when the Ming Dynasty was established, the north wall was pulled down and rebuilt five *li* to the south. In 1419, the south wall was pulled down and rebuilt more than a *li* farther south, forming the inner city as we know it today. The outer city wall was built in 1553.

instead!"

The Emperor saw reason in this. Beijing could only be built by a genius with knowledge of heaven and earth, who knew the ways of both the spirits above and the devils below. So he asked his advisers,

"Which of you can go and build a northern capital for me?"

His advisers eyed each other, not daring to utter a word, until finally someone really had to answer and Chief Adviser Liu Bowen volunteered, "I'll go!"

At once Deputy Adviser Yao Guangxiao volunteered, "And so will I."

The Emperor was pleased, sure that these two outstanding advisers had the ability to overcome dragons and tigers. He forthwith sent them off to build Beijing.

Liu Bowen and Yao Guangxiao took the imperial edict and travelled to the Waste where Beijing now stands. After putting up in a hostel, they went out every day to survey the terrain and figure out how to build the city in such a way that the dragons could not make trouble. However, Chief Adviser Liu and Deputy Adviser Yao had nothing but contempt for each other.

"Deputy Adviser Yao," proposed Liu, "let's live apart, you in the west city, I in the east. Each of us must think up a plan, then in ten days' time we'll meet and, sitting back to back, draw our plans for the city. Then we'll compare the two to see if they tally."

Yao Guangxiao knew perfectly well that Liu Bowen hoped to shine and hog all the credit.

"Very well," he said with a grim smile. "You're right, chief adviser. That's what we should do."

So the two advisers split up. For the first couple of days, although the two of them were staying apart and neither went out to survey the terrain, both heard a voice saying, "Just copy me and you'll do fine." The voice sounded like a child's, and the words were clearly repeated time and again. Who could the speaker be? There was no one to be seen. "Just copy me" — what did that mean? Neither adviser could make head or tail of this.

On the third day they both went out to survey the terrain again. Wherever Adviser Liu went he saw a child in a red jacket and short pants walking ahead of him. When Liu speeded up, so did the child; when he slowed down, so did the child. At first he paid no special attention to this, but then he started wondering about it. He delibertely stood still. Ah! How extraordinary! So did the child. Liu couldn't for the life of him think what the boy was up to.

How about Deputy Adviser Yao? He saw a child like that too, and couldn't for the life of him think what the boy was up to.

Back in their different hostels, again both advisers heard a voice in their ears. "Just copy me and you'll do fine." Liu in the east city and Yao in the west city wondered: Can this child in the red jacket and short pants be Nezha? Doesn't seem like him. Nezha was supposed to have eight arms. Liu in the east city and Yao in the west city came to the same decision: If I meet that boy tomorrow, I'll have a good look at him.

The next day, the fourth day after they had reached their agreement, Liu Bowen went out after breakfast for a stroll with an attendant. Why take an attendant today? So that the attendant could help him see if it was Nezha. Yao Guangxiao in the west city had the same idea. Both men had heard the same voice, seen the same child, and today they saw him again, still wearing a red jacket and short pants, but not the same jacket as the previous day: this one was more like a cape with a lotus-leaf edge, and from the two shoulders dangled soft silken fringes which rustled in the wind like arms. At the sight of them Liu suspected that this must be Eight-armed Nezha. He hurried forward to catch hold of the child and have a closer look; but the faster he chased him the faster the child ran away, repeating, "Just copy me and you'll do fine!" Then he made off and vanished completely.

When Liu's attendant saw him chasing down the road, he did not know what was up. He called after him, "Commander! Commander! Why are you running?"

Liu stopped to ask him, "Did you see a child in a red jacket and short pants?"

"Not I," said the attendant. "All this time I've been following you I haven't seen a soul."

Then Liu Bowen knew for sure that it was Nezha.

As for Yao Guangxiao, exactly the same thing had happened to him.

The two commanders went back to their hostels. Liu thought: "Copy me" must mean draw a plan of a city like Eight-armed Nezha, so as to keep down the dragons in Bitter Sea Waste. Fine! Let's see how you handle this, Yao Guangxiao. If you can't produce such a plan, you're not fit to be imperial adviser! Yao in the west city was thinking at the same time: Now we'll soon see you lose your title of "Chief Adviser"!

On the ninth day Liu sent word to Yao: "At noon tomorrow, in the centre of the city, we'll draw our plans back to back. Please be there on time." And Yao agreed to this.

At noon on the tenth day, in a big empty square in the centre of the town, two tables and two chairs were set out, the chairs back to back, and the two advisers arrived.

Liu asked, "Which way do you want to face, deputy adviser?"

Yao answered, "You live in the east city, chief adviser, so you should sit facing east. Your younger brother will sit facing west."

When they had taken their seats, attendants supplied them with paper, brushes, ink and inkstones. They picked up the brushes and stroke by stroke drew their plans. Just before sunset both finished their plans of the city, and each picked up the other's to examine it. Then both of them burst out laughing, because their plans were identical, each being an Eight-armed Nezha City.

Yao Guangxiao asked the chief adviser to explain his Eight-armed Nezha City.

Liu said, "This gate in the centre due south is Zheng-yangmen, Nezha's head. A head should have two ears, and those are the gates to its east and west. The two wells inside Zhengyangmen are his eyes. On the east side, the Chongwenmen, Dongbianmen, Chaoyangmen and Dongzhimen are four of Nezha's arms. On the west side of the Zhengyangmen, the Xuanwumen, Xibianmen, Fuchengmen and Xizhimen are Nezha's other four arms. The Andingmen and Deshengmen in the north are his feet."

Yao Guangxiao nodded, saying, "Yes, of course. But does Nezha have only eight arms — no heart, liver, spleen, lungs or kidneys?"

Liu Bowen's face turned red. "Of course he has!" he retorted. "How could a dead Nezha keep down vicious dragons?" He pointed irately at his plan. "Look, brother. The rectangular Imperial City is Nezha's viscera, and Tian'anmen at its entrance is the way into his viscera and leads in the other direction to Zhengyangmen, his brain. The long, level road between them is Nezha's gullet."

With a laugh Yao Guangxiao drawled, "Don't get het-up, chief adviser. I can see your plan is most carefully worked out. The two roads running south and north on both sides of the viscera are Nezha's main ribs, and the alleys branching off are his lesser ribs — right? You've really worked it out to the last detail!"

Although provoked, Liu Bowen had to keep his temper. At any rate, the plan for an Eight-armed Nezha City had been drawn, and neither adviser could hog all the credit. Chief Adviser Liu did not mind about this, but Deputy Adviser Yao became so cast down that he went off to live as a monk, waiting to see how Liu would build Beijing.

What Liu Bowen did not foresee was that the building of Beijing would enrage the vicious dragons, which led to Gao Liang's Race for Water and many other stories.

Gao Liang's Race for Water

HUNDREDS of thousands of years ago, so the old folk in Beijing say, this place was in a bad way because it was a briny sea known as Bitter Sea Waste; and people had to live in the western and northern hills, leaving the Bitter Sea to the Dragon King. The Dragon King, his wife, son, daughter-in-law and grandchildren lorded it over the Bitter Sea so that the local people who had taken to the hills lived a wretched life. How wretched was their life? They used the earth as their cauldrons and weighed out their firewood in bushels.

Some years later a boy called Nezha appeared in a red jacket and short pants. He had real ability. Coming to the Bitter Sea he fought the Dragon King for nine times nine days, eighty-one days in all. He captured the Dragon King and his wife, while their son, daughter-in-law and grandchildren fled. After the capture of the Dragon King the water slowly ebbed away and soil emerged. Nezha sealed up the different outlets to the sea, sealing up the Dragon King and his wife in a large lake, then built a big white pagoda so that ever after they had to stay there to guard it.

Now that the water had ebbed away, the name Bitter Sea was changed to the Waste. As time went by people built houses and settled down there. Viilages sprang up, as well as market towns. By now the dragon's son who had fled had become the king, and he and his wife took refuge with their son and daughter in a lake at the foot of the Western Hills. There they lay low, keeping quiet. When they saw the people of Bitter Sea Waste increasing from day to day, that increased their exasperation. They kept wanting to go out and rampage, to flood this Waste which was no longer called the Bitter Sea.

One day the new Dragon King heard that a city called Beijing was to be built in the Waste. That really enraged him. He thought: You people razed our Dragon Palace, and now you want to build a city there just to infuriate me! Then came word that Liu Bowen and Yao Guangxiao had back to back drawn a plan of Beijing — an Eight-armed Nezha City with eight gates — and its construction had already started.

The Dragon King told his wife, "Confound it! How maddening! If they build an Eight-armed Nezha City, we've no hope of making a comeback!"

"Never mind," said his wife. "Let them build their city. We'll stay here in our Dragon Palace and keep out of trouble."

The Dragon King stamped his foot. "That's no way to talk," he fumed. "How can I watch them sitting pretty! I must seize this chance, before their city is finished, to drain away all its water. Then before they can finish it they'll die of thirst!"

His wife, unable to talk him out of this, had to go along with him.

Having hatched their plot, the next day at dawn they set out with their son and daughter and a wheelbarrow loaded with vegetables. They had dressed like peasants going to the market in town. The Dragon King pushed the barrow, his wife pulled the loop in front, and with their children following some way behind they sneaked into Beijing. Of course the Dragon King had no intention of selling vegetables. He found an out-of-the-way spot and dumped them all there. Then he, his wife, Dragon Boy and Dragon Girl went round the town according to their plan. Dragon Boy drank all the sweet water there, Dragon Girl all the bitter water; then they changed themselves into two fish: scale water-panniers and lay down one on each side of the wheelbarrow. With the Dragon King pushing and his wife pulling it, they went out of Xizhimen bold as brass.

Meantime what of Liu Bowen? Now that the Eight-armed Nezha City had been built, he had taken his inspectors to supervise the building of the imperial palace. Suddenly someone dashed over covered with sweat. "Report, chief adviser!" he shouted. "We're in big trouble. Every single well, large or small, in Beijing is dry. What's to be done?"

Liu Bowen was flabbergasted. Then he figured: Everyone knows that the Dragon King, his wife and their son Prince Dragon are jealous of this city. Because of course once it's built, that tribe of dragons can never make a comeback. He

promptly sent subordinates to all the city gates to investigate and find out from the wardens if any suspicious characters had been through their gates that day. Horsemen galloped off to carry out his orders. Very soon they came back and reported that the only suspicious characters to leave the city had gone through Xizhimen. One of them reported, "An old hunchback was seen at Xizhimen pushing a wheelbarrow, with an old woman tugging in front. On the barrow were two dripping fish-scale water-panniers. They left by Xizhimen an hour ago."

The warden added, "They were such strange fish-scale panniers that I had a good look at them. They weren't too big, yet that old fellow was sweating as he pushed the barrow."

Liu Bowen nodded. "The vicious old dragon!" he said. "We'll just have to send someone to catch him and bring back the water."

The chief inspector asked, "How can we do that?"

Liu told him, "It'll be hard or easy, depending on how you look at it. Hard, because if that damned dragon sees someone after him, he'll swamp him with water to drown him. Easy, because if our man spears the fish-scale panniers then dashes straight back without looking round no matter if all hell breaks loose behind, once he reaches Xizhimen he'll be safe and sound."

His men shook their heads saying, "That's a tall order. Not easy."

Liu stamped impatiently. "There's no time to be lost! We

can't wait for that damned dragon to empty all that water into his lake, or we'll never get it back. Who'll take this on?"

His officers, high and low, eyed each other in silence. The chief adviser was frantic! Then they heard a clear voice ring out:

"Let me go, sir. I promise to catch up with the damned dragon and to spear the fish-scale panniers. I guarantee to bring the water back."

Liu saw it was a builder in his twenties, big-eyed and alert-looking.

"What's your name?" he asked, very pleased.

"I'm Gao Liang, a mason working on the palace."

Liu nodded and promptly took a red-tasselled spear from the weapon rack. He handed it to Gao Liang, saying, "Be very careful. I'll take troops on to the West Gate to back you up."

Gao Liang took the spear, promising, "You can count on me, sir." Then without one backward glance he flew off in pursuit of the dragon.

Once out of Xizhimen a dilemma faced him. To the north was a road to the northwest, leading to Jade Spring Hill. To the west was a road to the southwest, leading to the Western Hills. To the south was a road south to Fuchengmen . Which way should he go? He must make a lightning decision. He thought: Didn't Liu Bowen say that damned dragon is taking the water to his lake? The only lake is at Jade Spring Hill. I'll catch him before he gets there. He sprinted off to the northwest, gripping his spear, his eyes flashing fire. Before long he came to a gully between two high banks, just wide enough for a wheelbarrow to pass through, but too narrow for a horsecart. There were roads on both sides, however. Would the dragons have taken one of them? On one bank some peasants were talking.

One said, "Very odd they were, those two water-panniers glinting like the scales of a fish or dragon."

"Beats me," said another. "With all that sweet water in Jade Spring, why lug those two panniers of water northwest?"

Another said, "That old fellow and his wife were puffing and blowing, lugging that barrow of water so fast through our gully. At their age too — they're really tough!"

Gao Liang knew then that the dragons had headed northwest. Without a word, gripping his spear, he hurried northwest through the gully. Before long the road forked in front of a willow copse. Which way had the dragons gone? He was at a loss when he heard some boys in the copse.

"Hey, big brother with the tasselled spear, give us a drill!" one called to him.

Gao Liang saw some small boys beneath the trees clapping their hands and grinning. His spirits rose. He told them, "Little brothers, I'll drill you presently. First tell me if an old man and old woman passed here pushing a wheelbarrow."

"They took that track to the left," the little boys chorused.

Thanking them, he set off again. Later on this place was given the name Big Willows.

Hurrying on in pursuit, Gao Liang came to a pool that had dried up. Its banks were spattered with water, and in the bed of the pool was a rut made by a barrow. At once he understood: This must have been a pond. That damned dragon's barrow stopped here, and he didn' t leave a single drop of water — he carried it all away! Later this place was given the name South Hollow.

Planting his spear in the ground, Gao Liang vaulted over the pond and hurried on, eager to get back the water for the city. Before long he came to another pond — later called Middle Hollow — with a deep rut made by the barrow and many footprints. He realized that the dragons must be tired; why else should they have left so many deep footprints? If he put on a spurt he could certainly catch up. He bounded forward, and very soon Jade Spring Hill came into sight. Gao Liang strained his eyes. In the distance, sure enough, was a barrow loaded with two water-panniers. An old hunchback and an old woman were seated on the ground mopping their sweaty faces. They must be the Dragon King and his wife, quite worn out. Gao Liang exulted, his heart going pit-a-pat. He ducked into a field of sorghum to make a detour behind the dragons, then sprang up and speared one of the fish-scale panniers. Water came flooding out. But before he could spear the second, it changed into a pot-bellied youngster, who dived into the Jade Spring. The dragon's wife picked up the pannier Gao Liang had speared and flew over the peak of North Hill to escape to Black Dragon Lake. All these things happened at once, as fast as lightning. Before Gao Liang could decide what to do, the Dragon King roared, "You've ruined my grand scheme, damn you! Don't think you can get away."

With a start Gao Liang took to his heels, pursued by what sounded like a racing tide. When he speeded up, so did the water; when he slowed down, it slowed down too. Now Xizhimen came in sight, and he could distinctly see Liu Bowen above it. In his relief he forgot himself and looked round, and the water swept him away.

Since then there has been water in Beijing's wells, but most of it is brackish. What of the sweet water? It was carried off by Dragon Boy to Jade Spring Hill. And the Dragon King? That's another story. Later, over the place where Gao Liang drowned, men built the Gao Liang Qiao.* People seeing this stone bridge may pass on this story.

---

* A stream flows from the Jade Spring past Kunming Lake to the canal, formerly known as Gaoliang Stream, which runs southeast past the Beijing Zoo and the back of the Exhibition Hall, then east to Gao Liang Qiao. For thousands of years this was Beijing's main waterway, and before the Yongding River was diverted it was Beijng's main source of water.

图书在版编目（CIP）数据

北京旅游点的传说／熊振儒等编译. —北京：外文出版社, 2004
（熊猫丛书）
ISBN 7-119-03749-8

Ⅰ. 北… Ⅱ. 熊… Ⅲ. 英语－语言读物，民间故事 Ⅳ. H319.4: I
中国版本图书馆 CIP 数据核字(2004)第 065760 号

外文出版社网址：
http://www.flp.com.cn
外文出版社电子信箱：
info@flp.com.cn
sales@flp.com.cn

熊猫丛书
北京旅游点的传说

译　　　者　熊振儒等
责任编辑　陈海燕　李　芳
封面设计　姚　波
印刷监制　冯　浩
出版发行　外文出版社
社　　　址　北京市百万庄大街 24 号　　邮政编码　100037
电　　　话　(010) 68320579 (总编室)
　　　　　　(010) 68329514 / 68327211 (推广发行部)
印　　　刷　三河汇鑫印务有限公司
经　　　销　新华书店／外文书店
开　　　本　36 开
印　　　数　0001 － 5000 册　　　　印　张　6.75
版　　　次　2005 年第 1 版第 1 次印刷
装　　　别　平
书　　　号　ISBN 7-119-03749-8
　　　　　　10 － E － 3626P
定　　　价　8.80 元